LISTEN TO ME! Part1

MY LIFE, MY STORY, MY TRUTH,MY HEART, MY WAY

ERICA NICOLE YOUNG

ISBN 978-93-5610-280-4

© ERICA NICOLE YOUNG 2022

Published in India 2022 by Pencil

A brand of

One Point Six Technologies Pvt. Ltd.
123, Building J2, Shram Seva Premises,
Wadala Truck Terminal, Wadala (E)
Mumbai 400037, Maharashtra, INDIA
E connect@thepencilapp.com
W www.thepencilapp.com

All rights reserved worldwide

No part of this publication may be reproduced, stored in or introduced into a retrieval system, or transmitted, in any form, or by any means (electronic, mechanical, photocopying, recording or otherwise), without the prior written permission of the Publisher. Any person who commits an unauthorized act in relation to this publication can be liable to criminal prosecution and civil claims for damages.

DISCLAIMER: *The opinions expressed in this book are those of the authors and do not purport to reflect the views of the Publisher.*

CONTENTS

BECOMING HER

ON NOVEMBER 23,1993 THERE WAS A BEAUTIFUL BABY GIRL BORN IN CHICAGO ILLINIOS AT MERCY HOSPITAL. HER NAME WAS DESIRAY LIN STRONG. DESIRAY GREW INTO A BUBBLY HAPPY SWEET CHILD. HER EYES GLOWED LIKE BROWN DIAMONDS AND HER SKIN WAS BRIGHT AS THE SUN. HER SMILE WOULD LIGHT UP A ROOM LIKE THE STARS AT NIGHT IN THE SKY. HER MOTHER JOAN AND FATHER DERRICK ARMSTRONG WERE MARRIED AT THE TIME WHEN DESIRAY WAS BORN. DERRICK AND JOAN MET IN AN APARTMENT COMPLEX IN ALSIP ILLINOIS. JOAN HAD MOVED THERE AFTER DIVORCING HER FIRST HUSBAND MARCELL BECAUSE OF HIS INFADELITYS ;AND DERRICK MOVED THERE AFTER MOVING AWAY FROM GRENADA MISSISSIPPII AND SERVING IN THE UNTIED STATES NAVY. JOAN HAD A SON ALREADY FROM HER LAST MARRIAGE HIS NAME WAS MARCUS. JOAN AND DERRICK MOVED INTO A BEAUTIFUL HOME AFTER MARRYING IN SOUTH HOLLAND ILLINOIS. SHORTLY AFTER MOVING INTO THERE BIG NEW HOUS JOANN WAS PREGNANT AGAIN. SHE WAS HAVING A SON

THIS TIME. DESRAY WAS FOUR AT THE TIME AND MARCUS WAS TWELVE YEARS OLD. I HAD NO AWARENESS OF WHAT WAS GOING ON I WAS STILL LEARNING THE WORLD MYSELF. ALL I NEW WAS HER STOMACH WAS GROWING AND SHE WAS EATING EVERYTHING AND GETTING BIG. AS A KID THAT I WAS I WONDERED WAS SHE GOING TO BURST. THEN MY BABY BROTHER WAS BORN SEPTEMBER 23 OF 1997 NAMED ZACK. WHEN ZACK WAS BORN THE ATTENTION OF BEING THE YOUNGEST WAS TAKEN OFF OF ME AND ON TO ZACK. I THEN REALIZED THERE WAS A NEW BABY IN TOWN AND NO LONGER WAS IT ME.I DIDNT LIKE THAT NOT ONE BIT. I THEN BECAME DISOBEDIANT AND REBELIOUS TOWARDS MY PEARS. MY PARENTS HAD STARTED TO DISCOVER AFTER ZACK WAS BORN THAT THEY WERE FROM TWO COMPLETELY DIFFERENT WORLDS AND THEY DID THINGS DIFFERENT FROM EACH OTHER. JOAN WAS A CITY GIRL FROM THE WILD HUNNITS IS WHAT WE CALL IT. SHE WAS MORE FREE SPIRIT AND CAME FROM LIVING IN A FACE PACE CITY ALL HER LIFE. MY FATHER DERRICK HE WAS A COUNTRY BOY AND WAS RAISED IN A HOUSE WITH SIX SISTERS AND 11 BROTHERS. HE FELT THAT A WOMAN SHOULD DO WHAT HER HUSBAND TELLS HER ,STAY HOME ,WATCH THE KIDS ,CLEAN THE HOUSE YOU KNOW THE TRADTIONAL WAY OF MARRIAGE SHE WASNT THAT TYPE OF WOMAN. HE ALSO BECAME CONTROLING IN HER EYES

AND SHE COULDNT TAKE THE BACK AND FORTH AND THE ANGER THAT HE HAD TOWARDS HER. SHE THEN SEEN HERSELF NOT ABEL TO BE HAPPY AS SHE DESIRED TO BE IN HER RELATIONSHIP ANYMORE. SHE THEN DID THE UNTHINKABLE AND DERRICK HAD NO IDEA WHAT HE HAD COMING HIS WAY. DERRICK HAD OTHER PROBLEMS AS WELL. HE LIKED ALCOHOL VERY MUCH. AT TIMES HIS ALCOHOL WOULD GET OUT OF HAND AND MAJORITY OF THE TIME IT WOULD BE THE REASON FOR THERE ARGUMENTS AND FIGHTS. JOAN PACKED ME ZACK AND MARCUS UP AND WE MOVED WITH ARE GRANDPARENTS ANNE AND ALVIN HOUSE ON 103RD AND MORGAN. I WAS THEN 6 AT THE TIME AND CONFUSED AT THE SAME TIME. ALL THOUGH I WAS A KID AND DIDNT KNOW THE DETAILS OF MY PARENTS RELATIONSHIP I STILL NEEDED A EXPLENATION AS TO WHY MY LIFE WAS NOW DIFFERENT. WE DIDNT HAVE AS MUCH SPACE AS WE DID WITH DAD AND WE HAD NEW RULES AND ATE DIFFERENT FOOD. WE ALSO SAW LESS OF JOAN AND I HAD NO CLARITY AS TO WHY THIS HAD HAPPENED. IT ANGERED ME EVEN MORE BECAUSE AT THIS TIME MY FOCUS SHOULD HAVE BEEN ON WHAT I WANNA BE WHEN I GROW UP AND MY FOCUS BECAME WHEN AM I GOING TO SEE MY DAD AGAIN WHY IS MOM AND DAD NOT IN THE SAME HOUSE ANYMORE. I HAD SO MANY QUESTIONS BUT I KEPT THEM IN MY HEAD AND INSTEAD

MY ACTIONS BEGAN TO SHOW HOW I WAS FEELING. WE EVERYTHING WITH DERRICK BUT MONEY COULDNT BUY JOAN HAPPINESS SHE WOULD NEVER LEAVE HERSELF IN A POSITION THAT WASNT HEALTHY FOR HERSELF FOR ANYONE NOT EVEN US. JOAN CARED MORE ABOUT HOW WE SAW HER AS ARE MOTHER AND WHAT WE SAW AND MORE THEN ANYTHING. SHE NEVER WANTED ANYTHING TO BE PRESENTED TO US AS WRITE WHEN SHE NEW IT WAS WRONG. SHE PROTECTED ARE EYES FROM SEEING THE UNSEEN OF HER AND MY FATHERS RELATIONSHIP. SHE RAN AND LEFT HIM TO PROTECT HERSELF AND TO PROTECT US AS WELL. SO JOANN SET OUT AND SEEKED HER HAPPINESS.

GRANDMA ANNE AND GRANDPA ALVIN HOUSE

NOW ME AND MY BABY BROTHER ZACK ARE IN A ROOM TOGETHER THAT WAS GRANDPA ALVINS TV ROOM . MARCUS WAS IN THE BACK ROOM OF ANNE AND ALVIN HOUSE, AND MOM WAS IN THE BASEMENT SLEEPING SOMETIMES. WE THEN HAD TO ADJUST TO THIS NEW LIFE STYLE. WE ALSO HAD A NEW SCHOOL WE WENT TO AS WELL. I REALLY HATED THAT BECAUSE NOW WE RODE THE BUS TO SCHOOL AND DIDNT GET DROPPED OF BY DAD ND PICKED UP BY HIM ANYMORE. WE RODE THE BUS CALLED MR.JORDANS BUS. MR. AND MRS. JORDAN WAS FROM THE NEIGHBORHOOD AND EVERYONE NEW THERE ENTIRE FAMILY AND RESPECTED THEM. EVERYONE ALSO TRUSTED THEM WITH THERE CHILDREN. THEY HELPED JOAN ADJUST TO THE DIVORCE IN A GOOD WAY. I LATER FIND OUT AFTER NOT SEEING MY DAD FOR SO LONG THAT HE WAS PAYING CHILD SUPPORT AND WAS SUPPOSE TO GET ME AND MY LITTLE BROTHER ONLY ON CERTAIN WEEKENDS AND DAY. THE CHILD SUPPORT CONFUSED ME EVEN MORE. WE STAYED WITH

ANNE AND ALVIN UNTIL JOAN EARNED ENOUGH MONEYON HER OWN TO MOVE US INTO OUR OWN PLACE WITH MOM. WE STARTED GOING WITH DAD FROM ANNE AND ALVIN HOUSE ON THE WEEKENDS AND HE WAS NOT THE SAME GUY ANYMORE AND EVERY WEEKEND AFTER THE FIRST WEEKEND WE WENT WITH HIM HE BECAME MORE MEAN MORE SAD AND MORE UNHAPPY. I SEEN THE PAIN AND HURT AND RADGE AND ANGER AND BETRAYAL IN HIS EYES EVERYTIME HE LOOKED AT ME. HE BECAME COLD AND MORE HEARTLESS THEN HE ALREADY WAS. WE HAD MOVED OUT OF ANNE AND ALVIN HOUSE AND I WAS JUST GOING INTO THE SECOND GRADE.

NEW AJUSTMENTS

I HAD JUST STARTED AT C.I.C.S LONGWOOD ACADEMY AND WHEN I TELL YOU IT WAS THE BEST DECESION EDUCATIONAL WISE JOAN HAD MADE FOR US. THIS WAS A CHARTER SCHOOL IT WAS NOT EASY TO GET INTO THIS SCHOOL THERE WAS A WAITING LIST. THATS WHEN I THEN LEARNED WHO MY MOM WAS. SHE HAD SOME TYPE OF MAGICAL POWERS THAT SHE COULD GET US IN ANYWERE AND GET US ANYTHING WE WANTED. SHE NEW EVERYONE IN THE CITY AND EVERYONE LOVED HER AND NEW HER AS CUPCAKE. I TOOK IT AS MY MOM WAS THE PLUG. I THEN MADE NEW FRIENDS AND LOVED MY NEW TEACHERS AND MY SCHOOL HAD MORE VARIETY OF LEARNING MATERIAL THEN MY LAST SCHOOL SO I WAS INTREAGED. I THEN NOTICED AS WELL THE JOAN WASNT HERSELF ANYMORE. WITH ALL THE WORK AND TIME SPENT AWAY FROM HOME AND US. SHE WAS LOOKING FOR SOMETHING AND I HAD NO IDEA WHAT IT WAS. MY BIG BROTHER MARCUS WAS IN 8TH GRADE AT THE TIME AND HE WAS THEN ABEL TO BE AT HOME WITH US MORE. MOM WOULDNT COME HOME AFTER WORK AS

MUCH ANYMORE AND I WAS STARTING TO WONDER WERE SHE WAS GOING WHEN SHE LEFT WORK. AS YOU CAN SEE I WAS THE NOSEY CHILD. I OBSERVED EVERYTHING AND SUCKED IT ALL IN. IT WAS FUN HAVING MACUS WATCH US WHEN MOM WASNT THERE. HE WOULD STAY IN HIS ROOM MAJORITY OF THE TIME BUT WHEN HE DIDNT HE WOULD PLAY GAMES WITH ME AND ZACK AND WATCH WWE RESTELING WITH US. HE WOULD TEACH US HOW TO DEFEND ARE SELF AND WE FOUND FUN IN LEARNING HOW TO DEFEND ARE SELVES.HE USE TO PLAY HIDE AND SEEK WITH US AND GIVE WEDGIES SOMETIMES. WE EVEN HAD WATER FIGHTS BUT MOST IMPORTANT MARCUS GAVE US LOVE WERE WE BOTH THEN LACKED IT FROM JOAN AND DERRICK. MARCUS THEN BECAME A FATHER FIGURE TO DESIRAY AND ZACK. THAT WOULDNT LAST LONG THOUGH, MARCUS THEN BECAME EYE CANDY TO GIRLS. HE WAS A VERY HANDSOME YOUNG MAN HE HAD LONG BRAIDS THAT TOUCHED THE MIDDLE OF HIS BACK. HE HAD A CARMEL COMPLECTION AND STRAIGHT WHITE TEETH, HE ASLO WAS A STAR ATHLETE HE COULD PLAY EVERY SPORT EXSPECIALLY BASKETBALL AND FOOTBALL. HE HAD MUSCLES AND WAS BOWLEGGED WHATEVER THAT MENT TO WOMEN AT THE TIME. TEACHERS AND GROWN WOMEN AND EVEN SOME OF MY MOTHERS FRIENDS WOULD THROW THEMSELVES AT HIM. AFTER HE GRADUATED FROM 8TH GRADE HE

BECAME SOMEONE ELSE. SO NOW WE HAD A SCHEDUAL. ZACK STAYED WITH GRANNY ANNE IN THE DAYTIME BECAUSE HE WAS STILL A BABY. ME AND MARCUS WENT TO SCHOOL IN THE DAYTIME WHILE JOAN WAS AT WORK I WAS IN 3RD GRADE AND MARCUS WAS NOW IN THE 11TH GRADE. MARCUS WAS PLAYING BASKETBALL AND FOOTBALL AND BECAME THE STAR PLAYER AND THEN I HAD NOTHING TO DO I WAS WONDERING WERE DO I FIT IN THIS LITTLE FAMILY OF OURS.JOAN THEN PUT ME ON A CHEERLEADING TEAM AND I WAS REALLY GOOD AT IT. NO IT WASNT MY DESIRE BUT MY MOM WATED ME TO DO IT BECAUSE SHE DID AND IF IT MADE HER HAPPY TO SEE ME CHEERING THEN I WAS ALL FOR IT. ZACK WAS GETTING BIGGER AND I WAS BEGINING TO DO CHOIRS MARCUS HAD STARTED A JOB AND WAS EVEN MORE NOT IN THE HOUSE. I LOVED BEING A CHI-TOWN CHEERLEADER IT WAS SO FUN. WE GOT TO TRAVEL TO SO MANY DIFFERENT STATES AND WE WON ALL THE TIME. I LOVED WINNING AND BEING AMONG A GROUP OF ALL BLACK FEMALES LIKE MYSELF AND WINNING IN A DOMINANT WHITE SPORT FELT GOOD. JAM FEST WAS MY FAVORITE THAT WAS THE STATE COMPETITION WE HAD.

BODY CHANGES

4TH GRADE CAME AND I BEGIN TO GROW BREAST. I GOT MY PERIOD THE DAY OF 9/11 AND I HAD NO IDEA WHAT WAS GOING ON WITH MY BODY. I FELT PAIN IN MY PELVIC AREA AND I HAD NO IDEA WHAT IT WAS I WENT TO THE WASHROOM AT SCHOOL BECAUSE I THOUGHT I HAD TO POOP I SEEN I WAS BLEEDING AND WENT AND TOLD MY TEACHER AT THE TIME MRS.POPE THAT I NEEDED TO GO TO THE HOSPITAL BECAUSE I WAS BLEEDING FROM MY COOTIE CAT SHE CHUCKLED AND SAID OH NO YOU JUST GOT YOUR PERIOD AND SHE GAVE ME SOMETHING TO PUT IN MY UNDERWEAR THAT LOOKED AS IF IT WAS A REALLY THICKNAPKIN WITH STICKY TAPE ON THE BOTTOM. I ASKED HER WHAT A PERIOD WAS AND SHE SAID MY MOM WOULD TELL ME WHEN I GET HOME SHE DIDNT WANT TO TAKE THAT FROM MY MOM. I GOT HOME AND LEARNED THAT I WAS BECOMING A WOMEN SHE EXPLAINED EVERYTHING TO ME EVEN THAT NOW I COULD CONCEIVE CHILDREN AND THAT I WAS GETTNG BIRTH CONTROL SOON. ME AND MY LITTLE BROTHER SHARED A ROOM AT THIS

TIME AND A COUPLE YEARS HAD WENT BUY AND HE WAS IN KINDERGARTEN NOW. I WATCHED HIM GROW FROM A LITTLE SEED INTO THIS BEAUTIFUL FLOWER AND YET I STILL ENVYED HIM BECAUSE HE STILL HAD ALL THE ATTENTION OF BEING THE YOUNGEST CHILD THAT I HAD ONCE HAD. DARKNESS CAME BACK AT THIS TIME AND BEFORE U KNEW IT MY MOM HAD MOVED ON. ONE NIGHT SHE WALKED IN AND IT WAS CHRISTMAS EVE AND SHE HAD A GUESS WITH HER IN ARE NEW HOME NOW. SHE NEVER BROUGHT ANYONE AROUND US SHE DID WHAT SHE DID OUTSIDE OF OUR HOME WE DIDNT SEE A REVOLVING DOOR OF MEN IN AND OUT OF ARE HOUSE UNTIL THIS YOUNG MAN CAME ALONG NAME TROY. TROY WAS THE PERSON SHE WALKED THROUGH THE DOOR WITH.SHE INTRODUCED US TO HIM AND I INSTANTLY GAVE OFF A IMPRESSION TO HIM THAT I WASNT INTRESTED. I TOOK ONE LOOK AT HIM AND I SAID TO MYSELF HE AINT THE ONE. TROY LOOKED LIKE ANYTHING BUT WHAT SHE WOULD TALK TO. HE WAS STRONGLY NOT THE TYPE OF MAN IMAGE WISE THAT MY MOM WOULD EVEN LOOK AT. HE WAS UNATTRACTIVE ND HE DRESSED LIKE A GEEK AND LOOKED AS IF HE WAS A NERD. I HAD NEVER SEEN HER WITH ANYONE LIKE THAT IN MY LIFE. HIS BANK ACCOUNT WAS WHY SHE LIKED HIM FURTHER DOWM THE LINE I SEEN. HE HAD ALOT OF MONEY. HE WOULD TAKE

HER ON EXPENSIVE DATES AND TRIPS AND SPEND ALL TYPE OF MONEY ON CLOTHES AND SHOES FOR HER AND US WE DIDNT KNOW HE WAS GIVING HER ANYTHING FOR US BUT HE WAS TAKING CARE OF US WITH MY MOM FOR ALONG TIME BEFORE WE HAD EVEN MET HIM.HE STARTED STAYING OVER AND SPENDING THE NIGHT MORE AND BECOMING LESS OF A GUEST TO OUR HOUSE THAT MY MOM HAD GOT FOR ME AND MY BROTHERS. HE SPOKE TO ME WHEN I FIRST MET HIM AND I NEVERS SPOKE BACK. THE GLOSSINESS FROM HIS EYES AND AND THE WAY HIS LIPS CURVED WHEN HE SMILED TO SAY HELLO TO ME, THE WAY HE HELLED MY MOM HAND AS HE WALKED IN THE DOOR AS IF SHE WAS A TROPHY AND HE WANTED TO SHOW HER OFF EVERYTIME HE GOT A CHANCE, ALL OF THESE THINGS WERE POINTS I LOOKED AT AS A 4TH GRADER IN WHO WAS DEALING WITH MY MOM. I WANTED TO PROTECT HER HEART

SCARED OF THE DARK

TROY BECAME JOANN MAIN FOCUS AND PRIORITY AND MY FEAR OF SLEEPING IN THE DARK CAME BACK. ONE NIGHT MY BIG BROTHER MARCUS HAD CAME TO SLEEP IN MY ROOM BECAUSE I FEARED THE DARK. I WENT TO TWIST JOAN DOOR NOB TO SLEEP WITH HER AND MY LITTLE BROTHER ZACK BUT TROY WAS IN THERE. SHE WOULD NEVER LET ME SLEEP IN THE BED WITH HER WHEN HE WAS OVER. SO SHE YELLED DOWN THE HALL WAY AND ASKED MARCUS TO COME SLEEP WITH ME BECAUSE I HAD A NIGHTMARE. HE CAME IN MY ROOM AND LITTLE DID I KNOW I WAS WALKING WRITE INTO ANOTHER NIGHTMARE EVEN WORSE THEN THE NIGHTMARE I WOKE UP FROM. MARCUS CAME TO SLEEP WITH ME AND HE TALKED TO ME BEFORE WE WENT TO SLEEP ALL THE TIME TO EASE MY FEAR. THIS TIME WAS DIFFERENT. HE PULLED A PEACE OF HIS BODY OUT THAT I HAD NEVER SEEN BEFORE BEING THE AGE I WAS. HE ASKED ME " DO YOU KNOW WHAT THIS IS?" I RESPONDED "NO WHAT DOES THAT DO? AND WHAT IS THAT? HE RESPONDED WITH PUT YOUR MOUTH ON IT AND GRABBED THE BACK OF MY

HEAD. I HAD NEVER SEEN ANYTHING LIKE THIS BEFORE AND HAD NO IDEA WHAT IT WAS, AFTERALL I WAS STILL A LITTLE GIRL. I THEN PUT MY MOUTH ON IT AND HE PROCEEDED TO TELL ME TO GO UP AND DOWN WITH MY MOUTH ON HIS PENIS. IT HAD NO TASTE AS I THOUGHT IT WOULD. HE THEN PUT MY MOUTH ALL THE WAY DOWN ON HIS DICK AND SHUVED MY HEAD ALL THE WAY DOWN ON HIS DICK. I CHOKED AND MY EYES STARTED TO WATER. I CHOKED AND AT THAT POINT I DIDNT LIKE WHAT EVER THAT WAS THAT HE HAD SHOWED ME. I DIDNT LIKE THE CHOKING FEELING OF HIS HAND AROUND MY KNECK AND OF ME CHOKING OVER HIS PENIS IS WHAT I LATER DISCOVERE THAT WAS THAT I HAD PUT MY MOUTH ON. IT THEN BECAME CLEAR TO ME AFTER THAT HAPPENED WHAT WAS GOING ON. HE CONTINUED TO COME IN MY ROOM EVERY OTHER NIGHT AFTER THAT AND MAKE ME DO IT AGAIN AND AGAIN AND AGAIN. THIS WENT ON FOR THREE NIGHTS IN A ROW AND MY MOTHER WAS IN THE NEXT ROOM SLEEPING WITH NO CLARITY THAT HER DAUGHTER WAS BEING TOUCHED BY HER SON RIGHT ON THE OTHER SIDE OF THE WALL. SHE HAD NO THOUGHT IN HER HEAD THAT MARCUS WOULD EVER DO ANYTHING TO ME LIKE THIS AND SHE NEVER KNEW BECAUSE I NEVER KNEW WHAT WAS EVEN HAPPENING TO ME. I HAD TO STOP THIS BEFORE IT WENT TO FAR AS IF IT HADNT ALREADY. MY MOM

SENT HIM TO MY ROOM FOR THE FOURTH NIGHT AND WHEN HE CAME TO THAT DOOR HE WAS SHIT OUT OF LUCK. DESIRAY WASNT SUCKIN NO DICK TONIGHT AND HE SEEN THAT WHEN HE WIGGLED MY DOOR NOB AND THE DOOR WAS LOCKED AND HE COULDNT GET IN MY ROOM. MY FEAR OF DARKNESS HAD WENT AWAY AFTER ALL WHATS TO FEAR WHEN SOMETHING MORE SCARY THEN THE DARK WAS HAPPENING TO ME. AFTER THAT DARKNESS WAS FEAR NO MORE I TOOK A LIKEING MORE INTO BOYS. I THEN BECAME MORE CURIOUS OF WHAT ELSE COULD THAT THING THAT MARCUS HAD ME SUCK DO. I WAS NEVER THE SAME LITTLE GIRLANYMORE AFTER I STOPPED MARCUS AND HE WAS NEVER THE SAME EITHER. MY INNOCENTS HAD BEEN TAKEN AWAY AND BY SOMEONE WHO WAS A FATHER FIGURE TO ME, MY BESTFRIEND, MY BIG BROTHER. HE BEGAN WORKING MORE SO HE WASNT AT HOME AS MUCH AT ALL SO I DIDNT HAVE TO SEE HIM AS MUCH EVEN THOUGH I STILL WANTED TO SEE HIM AND HAD NO GRUDGE TOWARD HIM THE DISTANCE BETWEEN ME AND MARCUS GREW BIGGER. WE ALWAYS STILL LOVED EACH OTHER THOUGH. HE JUST IGNORED THE FACT THAT HE HAD TOUCHED ME AND SO DID I.MY MOM BROTHER MOVED ACROSS THE STREET FROM US AND HIS WIFE AND THERE KIDS.

UNCLE REMY AND AUNTIE TAHEENA HOUSE

MY UNCLE NAME WAS REMY H AND HIS WIFE NAME WAS TATA. THEY WERE MY FAVORITE TWO SIBLINGS HOUSE TO GO TO. THEY HAD TWO ADOPTED CHILDREN AND TWO OF THERE OWN. ALL TOGETHER THEY HAD FOUR KIDS ME AND HIS BABY GIRL IVY WAS THE CLOSES AND MY LTLLE BROTHER AND HER LITTLE BROTHER BLAKE WERE CLOSE AS WELL. AUNT TATA MOM LIVED WITH THEM AND SO DID AUNT TATA YOUNGEST SISTER WHO WAS ONE OF MY BEST FRIENDS GROWING UP AS A KID. HER SISTER NAME WAS PRINCESS AND SHE WAS SOOOOOOO FUN AND COOL TO ME. SHE HAD THIS SINCE OF FASHION THAT I LOVED AND SHE WAS A SHORT CHOCOLATE GIRL WITH PRETTY DIMPLES IN HER JUICY CHEEK BONES. ME HER AND IVY USE TO PLAY HOUSE, DRESS UP, DOCTOR AND SOME MORE LITTLE IMAGINARY KIDS PLAY. WE ALWAYS ATE REALLY GOOD FOOD WHEN WE WENT OVER THERE HOUSE AND I ENJOYED EVERY BITE. WE ALL SLEPT TOGETHER IN ONE ROOM AND NEVER WENT TO SLEEP UNTIL THREE A.M

SOMETIMES WE WOULDNT SLEEP AT ALL AND BE UP TO THE SUN CAME UP. WE LOVED TO PLAY TOGETHER AND THAT WAS MY FAVORITE PLACE TO GO AS A CHILD I DIDNT HAVE TO GET YELLED AT, I WAS SAFE, AND ALSO I HAD OTHER PEOPLE TO PLAY WITH. UNCLE REMY WAS ALWAYS MY MOM FAVORITE BROTHER BECAUSE OF HOW FREE HE LRT US BE IN HIS HOME. I WAS GETTING A BREAK AWAY FROM MOM AND IT FELT GOOD SINCE SHE WAS ALWAYS FRUSTRATED BECAUSE OF BILLS. SO I NEVER BIT BACK I RAN TO THE CHANCE TO ALWAYS BE A KID AND A GOOD ONE AT THAT.

PAPA ALVIN DIED SO DID SHE

MY MOM CARED ALOT ABOUT WHAT OTHERS THOUGHT OF HER. SHE COULDNT HAVE A KID THAT WAS DISOBEDIANT OR GOT IN TROUBLE AND DIDNT HAVE STRAIGHT A'S. HER IMAGE WAS EVERYTHING TO HER. JOAN WANTED THE BEST FOR HER CHILDREN AND IN ORDER FOR HER TO GET THAT SHE ALREADY KNEW THAT EDUCATION WAS GOING TO PLAY A BIG PART IN ALL OF THAT. SHE HATED TO SEE A C ON ANY OF ARE REPORT CARDS. I GOT A C ONE TIME AND SHE WAS NOT HAPPY AT ALL AND ENCOURAGED ME TO GET A BETTER GRADE IN A CERTAIN SUBJECT THAT WAS HARD FOR ME. ZACK ALWAYS GOT STRAIGHT A'SAND HE WOULD GET REWARDED FOR HIS GRADES IN FRONT OF ME. I WOULD GET SO MAD BECAUSE EVEN THOUGH I DIDNT DO COMPLETELY GOOD AS SHE WANTED ME TO BE I STILL HAD NO D'S OR F'S AT THE TIME. I FELT I SHOULD HAVE RECIEVED SOMETHING AS WELL AND THET THAT WAS FAVORITISM AT THE TIME AND BECAUSE MY OLDER BROTHER MARCUS HAD GOTTEN TWO F'S AND A D AND SHE STILL WOULD BE NICE TO HIM AS WELL. MARCUS WANTED MONEY SO THERE WASNT A TOY SHE

COULD BUY HIM OR HAD TO AS A REWARD FOR HIS GRADES. I WISH I COULD HAVE BEEN EQUALLY ENCOURAGED. I THENSTARTED TO THINK WELL I AM THE ONLY GIRL MAYBE THIS COMES WITH BEING A GIRL. WE DONT GET WHAT BOYS GET, BUT IT URKED ME SO BAD TO SEE THEM GETTING THINGS AND I DIDNT. I DIDNT WANNA BE A BRAT SO I WOULD JUST TRY TO BETTER. I FINALLY GOT THOSE A,S AND B,S AND SHE GOT ME SOMETHING. IT FELT SO GOOD TO SEE HER SMILE. SHE SMILED AS IF SHE HAD DID SOMETHING. ME BEING A KID AND NOT KNOWING SHE DID, SHE MOTIVATED ME WITH JELOUSY TO DO BETTER. THATS WHEN I REALIZED MY MOM WAS A STRATEGIC WOMEN. WE WERE DOING GOOD IN SCHOOL AND JOANN WAS LOVING HER JOB AND MANAGING BEING DIVORCED AND A NOW SINGLE MOM VERY WELL. THEN WE GOT HIT WITH A TUN OF BRICKS OUT OF KNOW WERE. GRANDPA ALVIN GOT SICK AND I WAS NOW IN 6TH GRADE. HE HAD THEN MADE UP FOR MY DAD BEING ABSENT AND TOOK HIS PLACE IN MY LIFE. I WAS A RANDPA GIRL, MEAND GRANDPA ALWAYS WAS THICK AS THIEVES. HE WAS THE ONLY ONE WHO EVER LISTEND TO ME EVER AND HE LOVED TO TAKE ME PLACES WITH HIM. HE WOULD TAKE ME TO SYLVAN LEARNING CENTER EVERY TUESDAY AND THURSDAYS THROUGH THE WEEK AFTER I GOT OUT OF SCHOOL IN THE DAYTIME. AFTER I FINISHED AT SYLVAN WE ALWAYS WENT TO

WENDYS AND HE WOULD ORDER ME AND HIM A JUNIOR BACON CHEESE BURGER AND A SMALL FRY WITH A CHOCOLATE FROSTY AND WE WOULD SIT IN HIS BURGUNDY OLD SCHOOL AND LISTEN TO SOULFUL MUSIC AND EAT AND TALK ABOUT WHAT WE WOULD SEE OUT THE WINDOW. HE WAS MY BESTFRIEND AND TAUGHT ME ALOT ABOUT THE WORLD AND LIFE. HE NEVER TOLD ME NO IN ANY TYPE OF WAY. HE ALWAYS TOLD ME NEVER TO TELL GRANDMA WE WERE EATING WENDYS BECAUSE SHE WOULD GET MAD AT HIM. I NEVER WANTED HER TO BE MAD AT HIM AND OF COURSE I WOULD NEVER TELL ON MY PAPA BECAUSE WE WERE JUST THAT TIGHT. YOU COULD NEVER SAY THAT MAN DID ANYTHING BUT KEEP A SMILE ON MY FACE. PAPA ALVIN ALSO USE TO TAKE ME TO 7ELEVEN WITH HIM SOMETIMES AND WE WOULD GRAB HIS PAPER AND HE WOULD GET ME AND HIM A SLURPPY. THAT WAS MY FAVORITE HE WOULD DRIVE AND SING MUSICE SONGS THAT WE LOVED TOGETHER. HE LOVED TO READ THE FUNNY STORIES IN THE NEWSPAPER TO ME AND HE WOULD READ HIS HORISCOPES AS WELL AS MINE TO ME. THIS IS THE REASON I STARTED TO CATCH INTREST IN ASTROLOGY. HE WOULD READ HOW MY DAY WOULD GO THAT DAY AND MY DAY WOULD GO EXACTLY THE WAY THAT IT WAS WRITTEN IN THE PAPER. I FELT IT WAS INTRESTING HOW THE STARS COULD KNOW SO MUCH ABOUT A HUMAN SOUL. I

THEN STARTED TO LEARN MY SELF THROUGH READING OF ASTROLOGY. WHEN DERRICK DIVORCED MOM HE LEFT US ALL SO MY GRANDFATHER WAS THE BIGGEST AND THE BEST HELP MY MOM EVER GOT FOR US. MY GRANDFATHER TOOK CARE OF HIS FAMILY HE MADE SURE EVERYONE INCLUDING MY GRANDMOTHER HAD EVERYTHING SHE NEEDED. WHEN GRANNY ANNIE MARRIED PAPA ALVIN SHE WAS A SEMSTRIST. SHE LOVED MY GRANDFATHER VERY MUCH. THEY HAD OLD SCHOOL LOVE IS WHAT I CALL IT. A UNDYING LOVE FOR EACH OTHER , A RARE FORM OF LOVE THAT ONLY GOD COULD GIVE A PERSON. OUT OF THERE MARRIAGE CAME FOUR BOYS AND A GIRL: ALL TOGETEHR THEY HAD FIVE CHILDREN TOGETHER. MY OLDEST UNCLE WASNT HIS REAL SON BUT HE NEVER TREATED HIM AS IF WASNT HE LOVED THEM ALL THE SAME. KEITH, KENARD JOANN KELLZ AND REMY WAS THE BABY BOY. MY GRANDFATHER STOPED TAKEN ME TO SYLVAN IN 6TH GRADE OUT OF KNOW WERE. HE ALSO STOPPED SLEEPING IN THE HOUSE, I NEVER KNEW MY GRANDFATHER TO SPEND THE NIGHT OUT ON MY GRANDMOTHER I FOUND THAT ODD. JOANN FINALLY TOLD ME WERE HE WAS AFTER SEEING I WASNT GOING TO STOP ASKING WERE MY PAPA WAS, AFTER ALL HE WAS MY DAD. SHE DIDNT LIE TO ME SHE TOLD ME THE TRUTH AND SAID HE WAS IN THE HOSPITAL AND HE WAS SICK. I ASKED IF HE

HAD A COLD OR SOMETHING AND JOANN SAID NO HE IS ILL BUT HE WILL GET BETTER. I SAID TO MYSELF I HOPE HE GETS BETTER I MISS MY WENDYS AND SYLVAN RIDES AND JUST SPENDING TIME WITH HIM. AFTER ALL WE DID EVERYTHING TOGETEHR. THAT WAS MY FIRST BESTFRIEND I EVER HAD AND I COULDNT IMAGINE LIVING WITHOUT HIM SO I CONTINUED TO THINK FOR THE BEST. MY FATHER WAS A BLUR IN MY EYES BECAUSE HE WASNT SEEN SO HE STARTED TO DISAPEAR OUT OF MY MIND AND I WAS OK WITH THAT KNOWING I HAD PAPA ALVIN. THE MORE ABSENT HE WAS IN MY LIFE WAS HELPING THE BOND BETWEEN ME AND ALVIN GROW STRONGER. MY GRANDFATHER WAS THE ROCK OF MY FAMILY, HE TOOK GREAT CARE IN FAMILY STICKING TOGETHER AND GRANNY AND HER LITTLE SISTER MAY WOULD ALWAYS GET IN DUM DISAGREEMENTS AND BE READY TO FIGHT AND THE MIDDLE BABY SISER MARSHAY WOULD ALWAYS INSTIGATE THE SITUATION BETWEEN ANNIE AND MAY. I WOULD GET A GREAT KICK OUT OF WATCHING THEM BICKER, BUT THE YEAR GRANDPA ALVIN GOT SICK IS THE YEAR THAT THANKSGIVING AND CHRISTMAS CHANGED FOREVER. IT WASNT A BIG FAMILY DINNER ANYMORE IT WAS JUST THE PEOPLE WHO LIVED IN THE HOUSE PRESENT FOR THOSE HOLIDAYS. ITWAS MY BIRTHDAY AND ALL I WANTED TO DO WAS SEE MY GRANDPA. JOANN BEIG THE GREAT

MOM THAT SHE IS SHE TOOK ME TO SEE HIM. SHE WON MY HEART BACK AGAIN DESPITE HOW I WAS ALREADY FEELING TOWARD HER. SHE ALWAYS MADE ME FEEL LIKE I WAS NEVER ENOUGH FOR HER NO MATTER HOW MUCH I ACHIEVED IN LIFE. I SEEN HIM AND WHEN I WALKED IN THE ROOM AND SEEN HIM, A PAIN I HAD NEVER FELT BEFORE CAME OVER MY BODY THAT I HAD NEVER EVER FELT BEFORE IN MY LIFE. I GAVE HIM A HUG AND MY BODY WAS COLD AND SO WAS HIS. I LOOKED AND HE HAD TEARS IN HIS EYES AND TUBES IN HIS NOSE AND HOOKED UP TO HIS ARM.I HAD NEVER SEEN SUCH A THING. HE LOOKED TIERD AND WEEK AND DRAINED. I HUGGED HIM SO TIGHT THAT DAY I DIDNT WANT TO LET GO BUT U KNOW HOW THE HOSPITALS ARE NO CHILDREN ALLOWED IN CERTAIN AREAS OF THE HOSPITAL SO I WAS STRIPPED OF MY LAST HOURS WITH HIM. I BECAME SAD AND MY CONFIDENCE IN MY SELF AND WHAT I WOULD BE IN LIFE STARTED TO LEAVE AS WELL. DECEMBER 18TH 2003 MY GRNDFATHER PASSED AWAY. I WAS DEVISTATED I WANTED TO KNOW WHY HE DIED NOT KNOWING WHAT DEATH EVEN WAS. I WAS THE NOSEY KID THAT STOULD AROUND THE CORNER AND EASE DROPPED ON CONVERSATIONS. MY GRANDFATHER HAD LUNGCANCER AND I HAD NO IDEA WHAT IT WAS I HAD JUST STARTED HEARING OF THE WORD CANCER BUT NEVER EXPERINCED WHAT IT WAS. ALL I KNEW THEN

WAS CANCER WASNT NICE TO ME AND MY FAMILY. EVEN WORSE MY GRANDPA DIED ON MY UNCLE KENARD DAUGHTER LAYLA BIRTHDAY. THE DAY MY MOM TOLD ME GRANDPA ALVIN WENT TO HEAVEN MY LIFE CHANGED FOREVER. NOW JOANN WAS MEANER THEN SHE HAD EVER BEEN TO ME, AND I WAS SAD AND ANGRY AND WANTED REVENGE FROM MY ONLY FETHER BEING TAKEN OUT MY LIFE. I FELT ROBBED OF A GOD CHANCE TO BE GREAT IN LIFE. I NEVER WAS AWARE YOU CAN DIE FROM BEING SIX AFTER ALL I WAS ONLY 12 YEARS OLD. I THEN HAD NO ONE TO TALK TO OR LOOK TO FOR ADVICE. HE WAS THE ONLY PERSON I TRUSTED WITH ANYTHING I WAS GOING THROUGH. I THEN STARTED TO GAIN A INTREST IN BOYS. WE STAYED IN THE HOUSE AFTER HE DIED WITH GRANDMA BUT HER AND MY MOM COULDNT LIVE TOGETHER VERY LONG SO INSTEAD WE MOVED AGAIN. I DINT WANT TO MOVE BUT GRANDMA COULDNT AFFORD TO KEEP TH EBIG HOUSE ON 101ST IN MORGAN SO SHE SOLD IT TO A FAMILY. WE ONLY HAD THREE MONTH NOTICE SO MY MOM BECAME FRUSTRATED TRYING TO FIGURE OUT WERE WE WERE GOING. ANNIE HAD MADE THAT DECISION ON HER OWN. WE THEN ENDED UP MOVING TO THE SUBURBS AFTER MY BIG BROTHER GRADUATED FOMR HIGH SCHOOL AND I WAS GOING TO THE SEVENTH GRADE. I ENDED UP LIVING FRIENDS THAT I HAD ALL

MY LIFE AND MY NEW FRIEND BREEZY I HAD JUST MET WE HAD JUST STARTED GETTING CLOSE AND IT HURT BOTH OF US TO PART WAYS BUT SHE STILL TALKED TO ME ON MYSPACE AT THE TIME. I HAD TO START ALL OVER AND WE ENDED UP SOMEWHERE WE DIDNT WANNA GO IN THE BOONDOCKS IS WHAT I CALLED THEM. MATTESON ILLINOIS IS WERE WE ENDED UP NEXT.

THE CHANGE THE MOVE

GRANMA ANNIE WENT AND FOUND HER A ONE BEDROOM APARTMENT AND MOVED IN BY HERSELF AND ME MOM AND MY BROTHERS ALL MOVED TO THE SUBURBS WHERE I THEN STARTED TO GO TO SCHOOL IN COLIN POWELL ELEMENTARY SCHOOL. ME AND MY MOM BOTH SHARED THE FRUSTRATION OF NOT HAVING A DAD ANYMORE. MY GANNY ANNIE HAD WENT NUM AND NO ONE NOTICED IT. SHE HAD BECAME SUPER QUIET OUT OF KNOW WERE AND BEGIN TO BE MORE TO HER SELF. SHE WAS LIKE A SECOND MOM TO ME BUT SHE CHANGED AS WELL AFTER SHE MOVED AND PAPA ALVIN DIED.HER SOUL MATE HAD LEFT HER AND SHE DIDNT WANT TO RE MARY TO ANYONE ELSE. SHE HAD NEW SHE HAD THE MAN THAT LOVED HER THE ONLY WAY SHE WANTED TO BE LOVED. SHE WAS NEVER THE HAPPY PERSON I KNEW HER TO BE WHILE ALVIN WAS ALIVE ANYMORE. I SNUCK OUT ONE NIGHT AND SOMETHING HAPPENED BADLY. I THEN WOULD SEE THE DARKNESS APPEAR IN MY LIGHT AGAIN. I DIDNT LISTEN TO ANYONE ANYMORE AND STATRED TO SWAY MY OWN WAY. I THEN LEARNED

QUICKLY THAT WASNT A GOOD IDEA. I SNUCK OUT TO AN ADULT AND HIGH SCHOOL PARTY BEING FAST. I WENT TO USE A RESTROOM LOCKATED IN THE UPSTAIRS BATHROOM OF THE HOME. IT WAS REALLY DARK AND HAD ANOTHER ENTRY IN THE MIDDLE OF THE STAIR CASE. AS I WENT UPTHE STAIRS I GOT PULLED INTO THE MIDDLE STAIR WAY ENTRY. A BIG HAND COVERED MY MOUTH AND TOLD ME THAT I BETTER NOT SCREAM AND I DIDNT. I THEN FELT HIM RIPPING MY CLOTHES OFF AND I STARTED TO TRY TO FIGHT. HE THEN TOLD ME THAT IF I SCREAMED OR FAUGHT HE WAS GOING TO KILL ME AND LEAVE ME IN THE CLOSET. SO I SAID NOTHING AND THERE I WAS GETTING MY INNOCENTS TAKEN FROM ME BECAUSE I WANTED TO DO WHAT I WANTED TO DO. I COULDNT SEE ANYTHING BECAUSE THE CLOSET WAS DARK JUST LIKE THE HALLWAY WAS. THE MUSIC WAS SO LOUD AND EVERYONE WAS DOWNSTAIRS THAT NO ONE HURD ANYTHING. AFTER HE FINISHED HIS BUSINESS HE RAN OUT AND I LAYED THERE IN PAIN BLEEDING AND CRYING. I HAD NO IDEA WHAT HAD HAPPENED TO ME AND WHY I CHOSE TO SNEAK OUT AND GO TO A PARTY. I THOUGHT I HAD SEEN THE WORSE WITH MOVING AND LOOSING MY GRANDFATHER AND THEN THE DARKNESS CAME BACK TO GET ME AGAIN. I DIDNT CONTINUE TO PARTY I RAN HOME FAST AS IF I WAS RACING IN THE OLYMPICS AND NEXT

THING YOU KNOW AFTER I WASHED UP AND WENT TO LAY DOWN MY MOM WAS WALKING BACK IN THE DOOR. I DIDNT TELL HER AND HAD NO INTEREST IN TELLING HER BECAUSE I DIDNT WANT MY BUSINESS TO END UP ON ONE OF HER MESSY FRIENDS THINGS OF STUFF TO TALK ABOUT. I WOKE UP THE NEXT DAY AND ACTED AS IF NOTHING HAD HAPPENED AND STARTED MY NEW DAY OF SCHOOL. NOW I HAVE A SECRET THAT I COULDNT TELL ANYONE BECAUSE IF I DID I WOULD GET IN TROUBLE FOR LEAVING IN THE FIRST PLACE.INSTEAD I BURRIED THE RAPE I EXPERINCED INSIDE MYSELF AND BRUSHED IT OFF LIKE THE STRONG WOMAN THAT I AM. I KNOW NOW THERE IS A SUCH THING AS BEING TOO STRONG AND THATS EXACTLY WHAT I WAS BECOMING. THE SOFT SIDE OF DESIRAY HAD LEFT. SHE WAS GONE A COLIN POWELL WAS ABOUT TO INTRODUCE HER INTO A WHOLE DIFFERENT WORLD OF STUDENTS. COLIN POWELL WAS LIKE A HIGH SCHOOL INSIDE OF A MIDDLE SCHOOL. I HAD WENT TO SCHOOL ON 95TH AND THROOP MY ENTIRE LIFE THAT MATTESON SEEMED LIKE A FAIRY TAIL TO ME. THE KIDS OUT IN THE SUBURBS WERE MUCH DIFFERENT FROM THE KIDS I WENT TO SCHOOL WITH AT LONGWOOD. I HAD STARTED TO EXPERINCE WHAT FASHION WAS WHEN I GOT THERE. I WORE UNIFORMS AT THE SCHOOL THAT I WAS GOING TO SO WE NEVER GOT TO WEAR REGULAR CLOTHES. I STARTED

TO SEE HOW OTHER PEOPLE DRESSED AND THE DIFFERENT COOL IDEAS THEY WOULD COME UP WITH WHEN DRESSING FOR SCHOOL. I BUILT A ESSENCE OF MY OWN SWAGG BY BEING FROM THE CITY AND SEEING HOW THEY DRESS AND NOW SEEING HOW SUBURB KIDS DRESSED I WAS READY TO BURST OUT INTO THIS NEW PERSON I WAS CREATING OF MYSELF IN MY HEAD. WHEN I STEPPED UP MY GAME WITH DRESSING PEOPLE BECAME MORE PERSEPTIVE TO ME AND INTERESTED IN GETTING TO KNOW ME. I THEN MADE IT MY GOAL TO LOOK GOOD EVERYDAY SO THAT I COULD STAY POPULAR. I THEN HAD MET FRIENDS OF A LIFETIME. KIANYAH, LORRY, MANDA, AND CASSY. THESE WERE MY NEW GROUP OF GIRLS I KICKED IT WITH AND WE CLICKED. LORRY HAD INTRODUCED THEM TO ME. LORRY WAS MY FIRST FRIEND ANYWAY, WE HAD GYM TOGETHER AND WE BECAME FRIENDS THEN SHE ASKED ME DID I WANT TO SIT AT THERE TABEL AT LUNCH. WE STARTED HAVING SLEEP OVERS AND WE STARTED HANGING OUT WAY MORE THEN WE EVER DID BEFORE. THATS WHEN THE BULLSHIT STARTED. MY MOM HAD LET TAY BACK IN HER LIFE AFTER ALL I DIDNT LIKE HIM FROM THE JUMP. THEY HAD STARTED FIGHTING AND LATER DOWN THE LINE I FUND OUT THAT HE HAD PAID A PRTION FOR THE TOWNHOUSE WE WERE LIVING IN AND HE WAS A VERY HONORY PERSON. IF HE LEFT HER OR DIDNT WANT HER

ANYTHING WAS FAIR GAIN FOR HIM TO TAKE IF HE HAD GIVEN IT TO HER. THAT WAS ANOTHER TRATE I HATED OF HIM. ALSO THE FACT I HAD TO LIVE WITH SOMEONE WHO I FELT WAS THE SCUM OF THE EARTH. AFTER ALL HIS KIDS DIDNT EVEN LIKE MY MOM BECAUSE HE WAS SECRETLY STILL CREEPING ON MY MOM WITH HIS EX WIFE. I FEEL HE SHOULD HAVE STAYED IN HIS BROKEN HOMEM INSTEAD OF COMING COMPLICATING JOANN SPACE AFTER SHE JUST LOST HER FATHER. ALSO MY BIG BROTHER MARCUS MOVED OUT BECAISE MOM AND HIM STARTED TO FIGHT TO MUCH OVER HIS GIRLFRIEND AND THINGS HE WAS DOING THAT SHE DIDNT ALLOW IN HER HOUSE. ALSO HE WOULD BE SELFISH TOWARD ME AND MY LITTLE BROTHER AND WOULDNT SHARE FOOD WITH US. MY MOM DIDNT LIKE HE DIDNT HELP HER WITH US AND STARTED TO LOOK OUT FOR HIS HIGH SCHOOL SWEET HEART MORE THEN HIS OWN BROTHER AND SISTER. HE ACTED AS IF WE WERE SOMETHING HE WAS ASHAMED OF. EVERYONE WAS SO WORRIED ABOUT THERE OWN LIFE I THEN STARTED TO DATE GUYS. I THEN DATED THIS GUY NAME SIBLEY HIS MOM DID HAIR AND HE WAS IN HIGH SCHOOL I WAS IN SEVENTH GRADE. SIBLEY WAS A G.D FROM THE 121ST AND EMERALD NEIGHBORHOOD. HE MOVED AWAY FROM HIS OLD NIGHBORHOOD AND LIVED IN THE BURBS WITH HIS MOM AND STEP FATHER.THEY HAD A HUGE BEAUTIFUL

HOUSE IN THE WOODGATE AREA IN MATTESON. HE WAS LIKE TWO INCHES SHORTER THEN ME BT I DIDNT CARE HE WAS CUTE AND HE MADE ME LAUGH AND HIM BEING FROM THE CITY MADE ME FEEL LIKE I WAS BACK AT HOME SOMETIMES. AFTER MY GRANDFATHER HE WAS THE ONLY ONE WHO PAID ME ANY ATTENTION AND GAVE ME ANY TYPE OF LOVE.MARCUS WAS GONE AND ZACK JUST PLAYED GAMES ALL DAY AND I WAS ON MYSPACE AND ON THE PHONE ALL DAY WITH SIBLEY. MOM WAS NEVER HOME WHEN WE GOT TO A CERTAIN AGE. I THEN STARTED TO FIND OUT DETAILS ABOUT SIBLEY AND HE DIDNT LOVE ME LIKE I THOUGHT HE DID. HE CHEATED ON ME WITH ALOT OF GIRLS AT MY SCHOOL EVEN GIRLS THAT I THOUGHT WERE LIKE SISTERS TO ME I LATER FOUND OUT TRUST NO BITCH AND LOVE NO ONE LOVE A GET YOU KILLED. I COULDNT BELIEVE HE WAS MAKING ME THINK IT WAS JUST ME AND HIM AND IT WASNT HE WANTED EVERYONE AND EVERYTHING. I COULDNT RISK HIM GIVING ME A DISEASE AND AFTER ALL I WASNT SEXUALLY ACTIVE BECAUSE OF THE FEAR OF SEX WITH HIM. NEXT THING YOU KNOW I STARTED TO HAVE FLASH BACKS ONE DAY WHEN I SNUCK SIBLEY OVER. AND MY MOM HAD NO IDEA WE WERE ABOUT TO HAVE SEX FOR THE FIRST TIME. I STOPPED MYSELF BECAUSE I THEN STARTED TO FEEL LIKE I WAS BEING RAPED AND HE GOT MAD AND LEFT. HE DIDNT EVEN

CARE ABOUT THE TRAUMA OR UNDERSTOOD THAT I WAS SEXUALLY ABUSED BEFORE. I JUST KNEW I WASNT READY.

THE SECOND MOVE

MOM AND TAY WERE FIGHTING MORE AND HE STARTED SPENDING LESS TIME AT THE HOUSE WITH JOANN. JOANN HAD CAUGHT HIM CHEATING ON US IN ANOTHER PROPERTY IN HAZEL CREST THAT HE HAD OWNED. HE WASNT COMING HOME AND STOPPED ANSWERING THE PHONE SO HER BEING BIG BAD JOANN THAT SHE WOULD BE SOMETIMES PULLED UP TO THE HAZEL CREST PROPERTY. SHE TOLD US TO STAY IN THE CAR AND SHE WENT TO THE DOOR. I THEN HURD HER SAYING SOMETHING ABOUT WHY DO U HAVE A SCREW DRIVER IN THE DOOR AND TO OPEN THE DOOR. SHE THEN WENT TO THE BACKDOOR WERE HIS COUSIN STAYED AT IT WAS TWO PARTS OF THE HOUSE. THE SECOND HOUSE WAS BUIKT INTO THE HOUSE AND HE RENTED TO HIS COUSIN HENRY. HENRY OPENED THE DOOR AND HE WAS TRYING TO BLOCK MY MOM FROM ENTERING THE HOME. SHE THEN GOT REAL STRONG AND PUSHED HIM AND SAID MOV HENRY! HE COULDNT HOLD HER I SEEN THEM DISAPPEAR INTO THE HOUSE AND I TOLD ZACK TO GET OUT THE CAR WITH ME I DIDNT WANT TO LEAVE HIM IN

THE CAR ALONE BECAUSE HE MIGHT HAVE TRIED TO GET OUT BEHIND ME. I WENT TO THE BACK DOOR I SEEN HER GO IN AND AFTER THAT I HURD SCREAMING AND YELLING. I RAN TOWARD THE YELLING AND SOUND OF THINGS BREAKING. I HAD NO IDEA WHAT I WAS WALKING INTO AND WHAT I WAS ABOUT TO SEE. THERE WAS ANOTHER WOMAN PRESENT WHEN I WALKED IN THE ROOM. CANDLES WERE LIT AND FLOWERS RED ROSES MIGHT I SAY WERE ALL OVER THE ENITRE DINNING ROOM FLOOR. HE HAD SEEM TO BE HAVING A ROMANTIC DATE. MY MOM WAS CRYING AND I HAD NEVER SEEN HER CRY OVER A MAN EXCEPT MY GRANDFATHER. MY MOM NEVER SHOWED EMOTION SHE THEN PROCEEDED TO LUNGE AT THE LADY BECAUSE SHE KNEW MY MOM ALREADY. TAY WAS A MASON AND THE LADY WAS A EASTERN STAR. THE LADY WAS ALSO UGLY LOOKED A LITTLE LIKE THE DINASOUR OFF DINASOUR TRAIN ON PBS KIDS ALL JOKES ASIDE IM SERIOUS SHE WAS ATTROTISH LOOKING. MY MOM FLIPPED THE TABEL OVER AND HER ME SAY MOM STOP AND WE LEFT. SHE LOOKED OVER AND YELLED DIDNT I TELL YOU TO STAY IN THE CAR AND SAID LETS GO!!! THIS WAS KNEW TO ME AND ZACK AND LITTLE DID WE KNOW THAT WAS THE LAST TIME WE WOULD EVER SEE HER SHED A TEAR. WE THEN MOVED AWAY AGAIN AND AT THIS POINT I WAS SICK OF MOVING. I THEN WAS IN THE 8TH GRADE AND

MOM HAD GOT A TWO BEDROOM APARTMENT IN ASLIP ILLINOIS. I THEN MET MY NEW FRIEND LILLY.WAS SO SPONTANIOUS. SHE ALWAYS CALLED HER SELF THE QUEEN AND WAS SUPER CONFIDENT IN WHO SHE WAS SHE TALKED ABOUT HERSELF AS IF SHE WAS THE SHIT AND CARRIED HER SELF THAT WAY AS WELL. I ENJOYED HER SO MUCH SHE WAS A FRIEND THAT BUILT MY SELFESTEEM BACK UP AND MADE ME REMEBER THAT I WAS FINE TO QUEEN LILLY WILL FOREVER BEA FRIEND OF MIND. WE BECAME THE BEST OF FRIENDS AND I WAS HAPPY TO BE HER FRIEND. WE LIVED IN THE SAME BUILDING THEY WERE ON THE SECOND FLOOR AND WE WERE ON THE THIRD FLOOR. HER LITTLE BROTHER PLAYED WITH MY LITTLE BROTHER ZACK AND THEY WENT TO THE SAME SCHOOL AS WELL. WE SHARED EVERYTHING AND WE EVEN WENT ON DOUBLE DATES TOGETHER. HER MOM ALLOWED HER TO HAVE A BOYFRIEND AT 14 BUT MY MOM DIDNT. SHE TRIED TO SHIELD ME FROM THINGS SHE KNEW EVENTUALLY WOULD HAPPENED WASNT READY FOR THEM TO HAPPEN. INSTEAD OF TELLING ME OR TEACHING ME HOW TO HANDLE MYSELF WITH GUYS OR GIVING ME THE PROPER PRECAUSIONS TO USE WHILE DATING AT A YOUNG AGE AND INFORMING ME ABOUT WHAT DATING IS AND SEX WAS SHE TRIED TO PUT FEAR IN ME ABOUT DATING. THAT DIDNT WORK OUT WELL FOR HER. HER SHIELDING ME

MADE ME WANT TO DO WHAT I WANTED EVEN MORE. I KNEW EVENTUALLY I WOULD GROW TO A AGE WERE I COULD GO OUTSIDE AND DO THINGS I KNEW I WAS GOING TO MAKE IT MY BUSINESS TO HAVE THE MOST FUN I EVER HAD IN MY LIFE EVERYTIME I WENT OUTSIDE.THEN THATS WHEN IT ALL STARTED. LILLY WAS DATING THIS GUY NAMED LAUPHYIAT. HE LOVED HIM SOME LILLY AND THEY WERE INSEPERABLE. HE HAD A FRIEND THAT WAS IN THE STREETS JUST AS WELL AS HE WAS. I HAD NEVER DELT WITH A GUY FROM THE STREETS BEFORE. HIS NAME WAS DEBO AND WAS FAR FROM THE TYPE OF GUYS I IKED. OH AND YEAH I SURE YOUR THINKING HOW DOES A 14 YEAR OLD HAVE A TYPE AT MY AGE WELL I WAS INTO B2K AND INSINK AND KINDA HAD A EYE FOR A CERTAIN TYPE OF GUY OH YEAH AND TYRESE GIBSON WAS MY FAVORITE ACTOR AT THE TIME AND I FOUND HIM VERY ATTRACTIVE. DEBO WAS LIGHTSKINED AND SHORT AND VERY STOCKY. I NEVER DATED A PERSON BASED OFF HOW THEY LOOK ANYWAY. I LOOKED FOR A GOOD HEART AND SOMEONE WHO WOULD ALWAYS MAKE MELAUGH. HIM BEING SUPER FUNNY IS WHAT GOT ME I LOVED TO LAUGH AND THATS ONE THING HE WAS GOOD AT DOING FOR ME. ALSO HE WAS A BAD ASS JUST LIKE ME. HE ALWAYS GAVE ME ANYTHING I WANTED EVEN WHEN HE COULDNT GET TO ME HE MADE SURE WHATEVER HE HAD FOR ME MADE IT TO ME. I

NEVER HAD TO DO ANYTHING FOR HIM AND HE NEVER WANTED ME TO DO ANYTHING FOR HIM. A THUG WITH A HEART OF GOLD IS WHAT HE WAS IN MY EYES. ONLY THING ABOUT HIM IS HE WAS TROUBLE AND I KNEW IT. HE WENT TO MILITARY SCHOOL WITH MY COUSIN AND HIS GIRLFRIEND ROMEESHA. I HAD FOUND OUT THROUGH THEM THAT HE HAD A GIRLFRIEND AND SHE WENT TO SCHOOL WITH THEM AS WELL. I HAD NO CLARITY OF THE GIRL UNTIL SHE JUMPED IN MY INBOX ON MYSPACE ABOUT DEBO. I FELT DUM AND LIKE I WAS FOOLED. I HAD FOUND OUT THEY HAD BEEN TOGETHER FOR FIVE YEARS BEFORE I EVEN CAME IN THE PICTURE. I HAD FELL SO DEEP IN LOVE AND I HAD NEVER THOUGHT THAT SOMEONE WHO I SPENT SO MUCH TIME WITH WOULD EVEN DO ANYTHING TO ME LIKE THAT. HERE I AM THINKING I WAS HIS GIRLFRIEND AND WHOLE TIME I WAS THE SIDE PIECE. I CONFRONTED HIM ABOUT IT AND HE LIED AND DENIED ANY ALLIGATION OF BEING WITH HER. SO I LEFT IT ALONE AND I STAYED AND THE GIRL LEFT HIM.SHE KNEW HE WOULDNT STOP MESSING WITH ME WHILE WITH HER SO SHE LEFT. LITTLE DID I KNOW HE WAS ON HIS WAY TO JAIL. AT THE TIME I WAS JUST A GIRL, NO ONE TAUGHT ME THAT IF A MAN CHEAT THAT IT WAS WRONG OR SOMETHING U SHOULDNT EXCEPT. AFTER ALL MY GRANDFATHER NEVER CHEATED ON GRANNY ANNIE AND MY MOM HAD TAKEN

TAY BACK AFTER HIM CHEATING ON HER SO I WENT OFF WHAT I SAW. I WISH I WAS TAUGHT TO LOVE MYSELF MORE BECAUSE THAT WAS MOST IMPORTANT. I THEN BECAME LOST IN THE DARKNESS EVEN MORE. WHEN HE WENT TO JAIL I WAS ALONE EMOTINALLY ON THE OUTSIDE. I WROTE HIM FOR A YEAR. I FELT LIKE I WAS MISSING OUT ON SO MUCH IN LIFE. HE CAME HOME AFTER THE YEAR HE DID IN JAIL AND I POPPED UP. I DIDNT EVEN GET A CALL LETTING ME KNOW THAT HE WAS HOME WICH WAS ODD TO ME. WHEN I POPPED UP AND CAME IN THERE WAS A GIRL IN HIS BED WITH A BABY. IT WAS THE SAME GIRL THAT HE WAS WITH FOR FIVE YEARS. I EVEN FELT DUMMER BECAUSE I CHOSE TO STAY. I DIDNT WANT TO DISRESPECT HIS MOTHER HOME SO I LEFT AND I DIDNT TURN BACK. HE STEPPED OUTSIDE AND STOPPED ME. HE SAID WAIT IM SORRY I SHOULDA TOLD YOU. I SAID TO LATE FOR THAT CONGRATULATIONS AND ENJOY YOUR BABY AND NEW LIFE. HE PROCEEDED TO SAY I STILL LOVE U AND I RESPONDED NO U DONT U NEVER DID U JUST USED ME TO GET BUY LIKE THEY ALL DO AND I LEFT HIM AND AFTER THAT DAY I WAS NEVER THE SAME. I BECAME A PERSON WHO CHOSE TO SAY FUCK MEN, BY ANY MEANS NECCESSARY I WAS NOT GOING TO LET ANOTHER MAN HURT ME. DEBO SHORTLY ENDED UP GOING BACK INTO PRISON ANOTHER 4 TIMES FOR ASSAISNATING

OVER 14 PEOPLE. I DODGED A BULLET AFTER ALL.

OVER 14 PEOPLE. I DODGED A BULLET AFTER ALL.

THE THIRD MOVE

NOW MOM IS NO LONGER DATING TAY AGAIN. THIS TIME WAS A LITTLE DIFFERENT BECAUSE BEFORE SHE MOVED FROM THIS APARTMENT SHE HAD GOT HER GROOVE BACK. SHE RAN INTO A OLD HIGH SCHOOL FRIEND. THEY WENT TO SCHOOL TOGETHER AND SHE USE TO ALWAYS TELL US STORIES ABOUT HOW HE DROVE THE NICEST CARS AND WAS FUNNY AND ALSO WAS THE BEST DRESSED IN THE NEIGHBORHOOD. HE ALWAYS HAD MONEY AND WAS A LOUDER TYPE OF MAN. SHE CALLED HIM ROWROW. I THEN HAD STARTED TO SEE ANOTHER PATTERN IN JOANN. SHE HAD JUST GOTTEN OUT OF A RELATIONSHIP THAT HAD HURT HER DEEPLY AND THEN JUMPED HEAD FIRST BACK INTO ANOTHER RELATIONSHIP. I CHOSE TO STAY IN A CHILD PLACE AND DIDNT SAY ANYTHING ABOUT THE FACT THAT I FELT SHE DIDNT LOVE HER SELF COMPLETELY. SHE WASNT EVEN AWARE THAT I WAS WATCHING HER EVERY MOVE AND THAT AS I GOT OLDER THAT I COULD POSSIBLY MIMICK HER BEHAVIOR IF I WASNT THE BRIGHT GIRL SHE MOLDED ME TO GROW UP AND BE. WE THEN MOVED TO 73RD IN TROY

AFTER LEAVING THE APARTMENT IN ALSIP. I DIDNT KNOW WHY WE WERE MOVING THIS TIME AGAIN. AT THIS POINT I DIDNT EVEN WANNA MAKE ANY FRIENDS ANYMORE. I GOT MORE FRUSTRATED ABOUT MOVING SO MUCH I HATED IT. I THEN BECAME A FRESHMAN AND HAD GRADUATED FROM HAMLIN UPPER GRADE CENTER. IM NOW A FRESHMEN IN HIGH SCHOOL, MY MOM TRANSFERRED ME TO ANOTHER CHARTER SCHOOL. C.I.C.S RALPH ELLISON HIGH SCHOOL. THIS WAS MY FIRST TIME EVER BEING IN HIGH SCHOOL I WAS A LITTLE NERVES. WE WORE UNIFORM AND WE WERE THE LIONS. MY SCHOOL WAS LOCATED IN GANG TERRITORY. THE SCHOOL WAS ON 80TH AND HOROY AND THAT WAS THE KILLA WARD NEIGHBORHOOD. BEST KNOWN AS THE 80'S BABYS. WE HAD TO WALK TO 79TH ST TO GO THE BUS. THEY ALSO HAD 079 KILLA WARD. THIS MAY SOUND CRAZY BUT THIS WAS THE SAME GANG AND THEY WERE ON A OPPOSITE SIDES OF THE STREET AND THEY ALSO WENT TO SCHOOL TOGETHER. SCOTT JOPLIN WAS ON THE CORNER OF 79TH AND HONORY. I HAD NO IDEA I WAS GOING TO SCHOOL IN THE MIDDLE OF A FULL ON GANG WAR. I DATED ONE OF THE 80'S BABYS KNOWN BY THE NAME JAMIE. HE WOULDNT CHEAT ON ME TO SAVE HIS LIFE AND WAS VERY OVER PROTECTIVE OF ME. TWO WEEKS LATER ALL THE GANG PROBLEMS WERE BROUGHT INTO SCHOOL. THE 079 BOYS WERE ALREADY GOING THERE BECAUSE IT WAS A

CHARTER SCHOOL AND BEFORE THEY BUILT THE ACTUAL SCHOOL CLASSES WERE HELD IN A CHURCH ON 95TH IN ASHLAND.THE 80 BABYS WERE LIVING IN THE NEIGHBORHOOD AND WANTED STUDENTS FROM THE NEIGHBORHOOD TO BE ABEL TO ATTEND THE CHARTER SCHOOL AS WELL. LITTLE DID THEY KNOW THAT THEY WERE RIVAL GANG MEMBERS THAT THEY HAD LET INTO A SCHOOL THAT 079 BOYS FELT THEY ALREADY RAN. EVERYDAY FOR THE PASS TWO WEEKS OF THE 80 BABYS TRANSFERING INTO THE SCHOOL PATTY WAGGING CPD CARS WERE PULLING UP AFTER SCHOOL LET OUT. I LEAVE SCHOOL AND I SEE A BUNCH OF OFFICERS WAITING TO LOCK ANOTHER BLACK CHILD UP. SO MUCH CRIME IN THE CITY AND YET THEY WANNA LOCK LITTLE KIDS UP INSTEAD OF MENTOIR THEM. WE WERE KIDS BUT YET I STILL SEEN THE POLICE FEARED US. THE GOOD LEARNING ENVIRONMENT HAD BEEN TAKEN AWAY ONCE THEY MIXED THE GANGS IN THE SCHOOL. EVERYDAY THERE WERE FIGHTS AND WE WERE SEEING MOB ACTION INCLUDING BLOOD SPLATTERINGS IN FIGHTS ALL OVER THE WALLS AND LOCKERS. WE HAD A VERY UNIQUE PRINCIPAL. DR.WILLIAMSON, HE STILL IS MY FAVORITE TO THIS DAY. HE BROUGHT THEM ALL IN THE LUNCH ROOM TOGETHER AND MADE THEM SIT DOWN AND HASH OUT THERE ISSUES AND COME TO A UNDERSTANDING. IT DIDNT STOP THE GANG

VIOLENCE, BUT IT DID HELP THEM STOP FIGHTING IN SCHOOL AND AFTER SCHOOL. THEY LEFT THE PROBLEMS ON THE BLOCK. I THEN SEEN MYSELF TURNING ITO A HOT MAMA. ALL THE BOYS WERE STARTING TO LIKE ME AND I WAS LOVING ALL THE ATTENTION. I HAD DATED THREE GUYS BY THE SND SEMESTER. I MET THIS GUY NAME ZELL AND HE WAS SUPER FINE LIKE OMARION FINE. IN FACT THATS WHO HE LOOKED LIKE AND HAD HAIR LIKE THE SINGER LOYD. ALL THE GIRLS LIKED HIM AND I NEVER LIKED A GUY ALL THE GIRLS WANTED BECAUSE I SEEN THOSE WERE THE BIGGEST CHEATERS. I WASNT GOING TO RISK BEING HURT AGAIN LIKE BEFORE. THAT WAS A HURT I NEVER WANTED TO EXPERINCE SO I BROKE IT OFF. I THEN STARTED SEEING MY PASSED HURT COME INTO MY CURRENT RELATIONSHIPS. I DIDNT TRUST ANY GUY AFTER WHAT DEBO DID TO ME AND SIBLEY. JAMIE WAS MORE OF TO MUCH IN THE STREETS THATS WHY I DIDNT WANT HIM ANYMORE I ACTUALLY WANTED TO MAKE IT THROUGH HIGH SCHOOL AND DIDNT WANT TO END UP DEAD BECAUSE OF SOMEONE I WAS DEALING WITH. I HAD A BLOCK UP ON MY FEELINGS AND I WASNT PLANNING ON TAKING IT DOWN ANY TIME SOON. I THEN STARTED TO WONDER AM I GOING TO FOREVER KEEP THIS WALL UP AND IF SO HOW WILL I EVER PASS.

DONT CALL MY BLUFF

AFTER WE BROKE UP HE STARTED DATING THIS GIRL NAME PUG AND SHE DIDNT LIKE ME NORE DID HER FRIENDS. FINALLY WE GET TO THE END OF THE YEAR AND HER AND HER FRIENDS DECIDE THERE GOING TO TRY AND JUMP ME THE LAST DAY OF SCHOOL. I HAD ALREADY GOT IN TROUBLE FOR BEATING A GAY GIRL UP FOR GRABBING MY BOOBS AND BLOWING A KISS AT ,E AND I HAD ALREADY GOT IN TROUBLE FOR FIGHTING A GUY THAT WAS SENIOR. I KNEW IF I FOUGHT THAT I WOULD BE UP FOR EXPULSION BUT WHAT I WAS SUPPOSED TO DO GET JUMOED BY A ARMY OF ANGRY FEMALES OR LOOK LIKE A PUNK. NEITHER ONE OF THEM WAS A OPTION FOR ME SO I HAD THOUGHT WHAT I WAS GOING TO DO ALL DAY LONG. I DIDNT EVEN CARE WHY SHE WANTED TO FIGHT ME AND STILL TO THIS DAY DONT KNOW AND GIVES ZERO FUCKS. WORD HAD GOT OUT THAT SHE AND HER FRIENDS HAD WANTED TO FIGHT ME BECAUSE I HAD BEAT HER FRIEND GEAORGIA UP ON HER BIRTHDAY. GEAORGIA HAD STOLEN MY BEST FRIEND PRINCESS AWAY FROM ME OR SO I THOUGHT SHE WAS MY BESTFRIEND. BUT

WHEN ME AND GEORGIA FOUGHT PRINCESS SHOWED ME WE WERENT FRIENDS AT ALL. THE BELL WRONG AND MY PLAY BROTHER TYRONE RAN UP TO MY LOCKER AND HOLLARD YOOOOOO SIS! I HOLLA WASSUP BRO WE WALKING TO THE BUS TOGETHER TODAY? HE THEN LOOKS AT ME IN PANIC AND SAID SIS DONT GO OUT THE BUILDING THEY TRYNA JUMP U. ITS 20 GIRLS STANDING AT THE END OF 79TH STREET WAITING ON U TO WALK THAT WAY. WHE I FOUNDOUT HOW MANY IT WAS I SAID WHY THEY NEED 20 GIRLS FOR ONE PERSON? I GUESS THEY WAS SCARED OR NEW I WASNT GONE BE EASY TO BEAT. HE THEN PROCEEDED TO SAY IM NOT GONE LET THEM JUMP YOU SIS IF YOU WANNA FACE THEM I WILL GO OUT THERE WITH YOU AND WE CAN WHOOP THEM TOGETHER. HE SAID HIM ME AND TAPPY AND BAYBAY WAS ALL GONE HELP IF THEY TRIDE TO JUMP THOSE WERE TYRONE FEMALE COUSINS. AND IF HE FOUGHT THEY ALL DID TO. THEY WERE FROM THE LOW END AND DIDNT PLAY AND LOVED TO FIGHT PEOPLE THAT WERE BULLYS. I WAS NEVER SCARED OF ANYONE AND I KEPT SOMETHING ON ME AT ALL TIMES BECAUSE I KNEW WHAT TYPE OF SCHOOL I WAS GOING TO AND I ALWAYS WAS TOLD NEVER LET A CHICK HIT ME OR SCRATCH ME IN MY FACE SO I WAS ALWAYS PREPAIRED. I SHOWED TYRONE WHAT I HAD AND HE LOOKED PUZZLED. MY MOM HAD LET MY BIG BROTHER MOVE BACK WITH

US AND HE HAD THEN BEEN WORKING FOR THIS COMPANY NAME SCHNEIDER. MARCUS WOULD BRING THE BLADES HOME HE USED TO CUT THE BIXES OPEN WITH. I HAD TOOK THREE KNOWING HE WOULDNT NOTICE BECAUSE HE HAD SO MANY JUST TO PROTECT MYSELF BECAUSE I GOT ON THE BUS BY MYSELF. I LET EVERYONE LEAVE BEFORE I WENT OUTSIDE SO THEY COULD GET IN THERE POSITIONS AND WOULDNT SEE ME COMING BUT ONE WAY. I WANTED THEM TO SEE ME COMING STRAIGHT TO ME. I FEARED KNOW ONE BUT THE LORD.THEY THOUGHT I WAS SUPPOSED TO BE SCARED AND I WAS FAR FROM IT. THEY WAS BETTER OFF JUMPING ME INSIDE THE SCHOOL INSTEAD OF LETTING ME GET A HEADS UP. THEY WAS TRYNA JUMP ME SO I WAS BRINGING MY PEOPLE WITH ME TO WICH WAS THE LORD MYSELF AND THESE 3 SWITCH BLADES I HAD IN MY HAND.I WALKED OUT THE DOORS AND STARTED TO MARCH ALL BY MYSELF TOWARD 79TH AND HONORE.THEY WERE STANDING WAITING AT THE END OF THE BLOCK LIKE I WAS TOLD THEY WOULD BE. I WALKED FAST AS I COULD TOWARD THEM AND BEFORE I COULD GET TO THE END OF THE BLOCK I HAD HURD SECURITY AND POLICE OFFICERS RUNNING DOWN THE SIDE WALK SAYING DESIRAAAAAAYYY! STOOOOOOOOPPPP, DONT DO IT! HE GRABBED ME THE SECURITY GUARD THAT ALWAYS WAS SENT TO GET ME EVERY SINGLE TIME I GOT IN

TROUBLE. HE SAID YO BROTHER TOLD ME YOU GOT SOME BLADES ON YOU I KNOW WHAT YOU THINKING DONT DO IT. HE TOLD ME TO GIVE HIM THE BLADES BEFORE THE POLICE GOT THERE. I SAID NO THEY TYRNA KILL ME SO IM ABOUT TO KILL EVERY SINGLE ONE OF THEM . THE GIRLS THEN STARTED TO DISPERSE WHEN THEY FIGURED OUT I HAD WEOPANS ON ME. I WAS ESCORTED BACK INTO THE SCHOOL. HE SAVED ME FROM MAKING ONE OF THE WORSE DECISIONS I COULD HAVE EVER MADE IN MY LIFE. I REALIZED I ALMOST THROUGH AWAY EVERYTHING BECAUSE OF MY PRIDE. MY DAD CAME TO PICK ME UP. I ASKED CAN I LIVE WITH HIM. HE SAID YES SHOCKINGLY. I THEN LEFT RALPH ELLISON AFTER THE TOLD DERRICK THAT I COULDNT GO THERE NEXT YEAR ANYWAY BECAUSE OF THE SITUATION. I TOLD MY DAD I DIDNT WANNA GO THERE ANYMORE ANYWAY BECAUSE I FELT THERE WERE STILL GOING TO JUMP ME WHEN I CAME BACK OR IF I CAME BACK THE FOLLOWING YEAR. SO THERE IT WAS I MOVED WITH DERRICK TO A BRAND NEW HOUSE HE HAD BOUGHT FOR ME AND MY BROTHER IN SOUTH HOLLAND ILLINOIS. MY MOM HAD STARTED DAITING ANOTHER GUY AGAIN AND I WAS OVER BEING IN HER HOME ANYWAY. WE WERE GETTING INTO ALOT OF ARGUEMENTS AND I STARTED TO FEEL LIKE THE CINDERELLA STEP SISTER. MY DAD HAD NO CLARITY THAT BUY LETTING ME MOVE WIT

HIM HE WAS TEACHING ME ITS OK TO RUN FROM MY PROBLEMS.

T.W.H.S YES!

I STARTED AT A NEW SCHOOL IT WAS MY SOPHMORE YEAR IN HIGH SCHOOL. I NOW WENT TO THORNWOOD HIGH SCHOOL. THIS SCHOOL WAS MUCH DIFFERENT FROM RALPH ELLISON. GIRLS WERE WEARING HIGH HEELS TO SCHOOL AND DESIGNER BAGS. I THEN GOT INTRODUCED TO A WHOLE NEW LIFESTYLE PF LIVING. I REALLY DIDNT FEEL LIKE I WAS IN HIGH SCHOOL UNTIL I GOT TO THORNWOOD. I KNEW THE CHEERLEADING COACH THERE BECAUSE ME AND HER DAUGHT JASMINE WERE BOTH ON THE SAME CHI-TOWN CHEERLEADING TEAM TOGEHTER. SHE WAS EXSTACTIC TO SEE THAT I HAD STARTED AT THE WOOD. I BECAME A CHEERLEADER INSTANTLY. I KNEW HOW TO FLIP AND SHE DIDNT HAVE TO TEACH ME ANYTHING BECAUSE SHE ALREADY KNEW MY BACKGROUND SO I WAS INSTANTLY ADDED BECAUSE I HAD IT LIKE THAT. I THEN BECAME A T-BIRD THATS WHAT THEY CALLED US. FROM GROWING UP AND BEING IN FASHION SHOWS FOR FUN RAISERS FOR THE CHEERLEADING UNIFORMS AND FUNDING EVERY YEAR. TO MEETING MY FIRST TRUE BESTFRIEND

DONEESHA. DONEESHA WAS A SHORT SPUNKY CUTE SQUINTY EYED LONG HAIR DONT CARE GIRL. SHE WAS LIKE ME BUT HAD GREW UP IN THE CSUBURBS. WE DID EVERYTHING TOGETHER EVEN BEAT UP FEMALES. WE WON 7TH PLACE IN THE STATE CHAMPIONSHIP CHEERLEADING COPETITION. THAT WAS THE FIRST TIME IN 25 YEARS THAT THORNWOOD HAD ENDED UP IN THE STATE CHAMPIONSHIP. THAT WAS THE LEAST OF MY CONCERNS THOUGH, I STARTED MAKING MORE FRIENDS AND GOING TO PARTYS OUTSIDE OF SCHOOL. I STARTED DRINKING AND SMOKING AND PARTYING MORE. I ALSO BEGAN TO SNEAK OUT THE HOUSE, THATS ONLY BECAUSE IT WAS EASY TO BECAUSE MY DAD WORKED AT NIGHTS SO THERE WAS NO WAY HE KNEW IF I WAS HOME OR NOT. I THEN GO BESIDES MYSELF AND THEN BEGAN TO SNEAK PEOPLE IN THE HOUSE IN THE DAY TIME WHEN HE SWITCHED HIS SHIFFS. I WAS ALONE ALOT LIVING WITH MY DAD. I STARTED DATING THIS GUY FROM THORNRIDGE HIGH SCHOOL ARE RIVAL SCHOOL NAMED J.T. I WAS WRONG BUT THEN AGAIN I WAS A TEENAGE GIRL WHO HAD PREVIOUSLY BEEN TOUCHED AND WAS LEARNING NEW THINGS ABOUT HER BODY PARTS. MY MOM WASNT IN THE HOUSE ANYMORE AND HER ADVICE ON SEX WAS DONT HAVE SEX BECAUSE YOU WILL DIE. I HAD WANTED TO KNOW WHAT THE FEELING OF LOVE WAS AND I WANTED HIM TO SHOW

ME. I TOOK HIS WORD THAT THE WAY OF SHOWING ME HE LOVED ME WAS TO GO INSIDE OF MY BODY SO I LET HIM IN. MY MOM NORE DID MY DAD GIVE ME HUGS ON A REGULAR OR TELL ME THEY LOVED ME ON A REGULAR THE OLDER I GOT THE MORE DISTANTS WITH LOVE TOWARD ME FROM BOTH OF THEM I SEEN GREW.. I THEN GOT CAUGHT BY THE NEIGHBOR WHEN J.T WAS LEAVING OUT SHE WAS PULLING IN. SHE TOLD MY DAD I HAD A OY IN THE HOUSE AND HE CAME HOME EARLY. I THEN SEEN A SIDE I HAD NEVER SEEN BEFORE FROM HIM, HE WAS ANGRYRIER THEN I HAVE EVER SEEN HIM BEFORE IN MY LIFE.I THEN STOPPED TALKING TO J.T AND MOVED BACK WITH MY MOM. BEFORE I CHOSE TO MOVE BACK WITH MY MOM I HAD A SUICIDE INSADENT WITH MY DAD THAT MADE ME NEVER WANNA SEE HIM AGAIN. EVERY DAY AFTER THE DAY I GOT CAUGHT WITH J.T MY DAD HAD BECOME VERBALLY ABUSIVE TOWARD ME AND MEAN. I COULDNT TAKE THE VERBAL ABUSE SO MUCH THAT I HAD TRIED TO HANG MYSELF WITH HIS BELT. AS HE WAS YELLING AT ME ONE DAY I TOOK HIS BELT AND CLOSED MY ROOM DOOR. I STOOD ON THE SPINNING DESK CHAIR I HAD IN MY ROOM AND STUCK THE BELT AT THE TOP OF THE DOOR BETWEEN THE CRACK OF THE SEEL OF THE TOP OF THE DOOR. I THEN JUMPED OFF THE CHAIR AND MY BODY SWUNG FROM THE TOP OF THE DOOR. THE TOP OF MY

TOWE NAIL WAS THE ONLY THING TOUVHING THE FLOOR. I FELT MY BREATH WEEKENING. THE ROOM WAS GETTING DARKER. THE YELLING AND SCREAMING WAS LEAVIN MY HEAD. AND THEN HE BURSED IN THE DOOR WHILE I WAS HANGING FROM IT AND I TOOK A DEEP HARD BREATH. I GUESS GOD WAS WITH ME AT THE TIME BECAUSE THAT MOMENT SHOWED ME I HAD MORE TO DO IN THIS WORLD. GOD DIDNT WANT ME TO GO. HE FELT MY FEAR OF DOING IT TO MYSELF ANYWAY. AFTER HE SEEN THAT I WAS GOING TO KILL MYSELF HE DIDNT LET UP ON THE ABUSE. HE SAID TO ME I QUOTE" YOU WANNA KILL YOURSELF? WELL LET ME HELP YOU!". AFTER THAT I NEVER LOOKED AT HIM THE SAME WAY. HE SHOWED ME HADNT CARED IF I LIVED OR DIED. IT ACTUALLY MADE ME WANNA HARM MYSELF MORE. HE HAD GOOD REASON TO SAY WHAT HE SAID BUT AT THE SAME TIME HIS APPROACH WAS COMPLETELY WRONG. SO I MOVED BACK WITH JOANN SHE WAS NOW IN BLUE ISLAND ILLINOIS. IT THEN BECAME HARDER FOR ME TO GET TO SCHOOL BECAUSE I USE TO WALK TO SCHOOL FROM DERRICK HOUSE. MY MOM MOVED CLOSER TO MY SCHOOL BECAUSE SHE KNEW I DIDNT WANNA LEAVE. MY MOM SACRIFICED FOR ME SO THAT I COULD HAVE WHAT I WANTED. WE THEN MOVED TO HAXEL CREST AND SHE WAS BACK WITH TAY. HE JUST COULDNT LEAVE JOANN ALONE. HE ALWAYS CAME BACK EVEN WHEN

HE WAS BEING A DICK HEAD HALF THE TIME. I STARTED MESSING WITH THIS GUY NAME EVEN AND THIS WAS MY JUINOR YEAR AND I WAS STILL AT THE WOOD. I STARTED DATING THIS GUY NAME EVAN AND HE WAS MY HOMIE LASHONDREA BIG BROTHER. ME AND EVAN BEGAN TO GET CLOSER AND HE SEEMED AS IF HE REALLY LIKED HIM I HAD STARTED TO LIKE HIM AS WELL BUT WE WERENT OFFICIAL SO I KEPT MY OPTIONS OPEN AND SO DID HE. EVAN WAS ALSO A OLDER GUY AND HE HAD USE TO GO TO THE WOOD AS WELL BUT HE HAD GOT KICKED OUT YEARS BEFORE I EVEN GOT THERE. I KNOW WHAT YOUR THINKING THIS GIRL AND THESE BAD GUYS. YEAH I HAD A THING FOR RUFF NECKS. WE THEN BEGAN HAVING SEX AND HE WOULD SNEAK IN THROUGH MY WINDOW SINCE HE LIVED TWO BLOCKS UP ANYWAY. HE WOULD SPEND NIGHTS WITH ME WATCH MOVIES WITH ME AND OF COURSE PLEASE ME SEXUALLY IN EVERY WAY. EVERYONE OF HIS FRIENDS KNEW ABOUT US BECAUSE THEY WOULD LIFT HIM INTO MY WINDOW AND COME BACK AND HELP HIM BACK OUT THE WINDOW. MY MOM HAD MARRIED TAY FINALLY AFTER 11 YEARS OF BEING TOGETHER ON AND OFF. HIS COUSIN HENRY KNOW LONGER LIVED IN THE BACK OF THE HOUSE SO IT WAS LIKE ME AND ZACK HAD THE WHOLE FRONT OF THE HOUSE TO OUR SELF. MARCUS LIVED IN THE BASEMENT BUT HE WAS AN ADULT NOW SO HE BAIRLEY

STAYED THERE. HE WAS STAYING WITH THIS GIRL THAT WAS ONE OF MY COUSINS BESTFRIENDS. SHE WAS NICE I LIKED HER. I THEN DISCOVERED NOBODY WAS REALLY PAYING ATTENTION TO US SO THATS WHAT MADE ME FEEL AS IF I COULD DO ANYTHING I WANTED. AFTER ALL I WAS LIVING LIKE A GROWN UP ANYWAY. FEEDING MYSELF AND DOING EVERYTHING IN MY HOUSE ON MY OWN. I SNUCK OUT ONE NIGHT WITH MY FEMALE FRIEND THAT HAD LIVED A BLOCK AWAY FROM ME. HE NAME WAS LACRAY. EVERYONE LIKED HER BECAUSE SHE HAD A BEAUTIFUL SILLY PERSONALLITY AND SHE HAD A BIG JIGGALY BOOTY. I LOVED HER WE WERE LIKE SISTERS UNTIL THE NIGHT I SNUCK OUT WITH HER. THIS NIGHT I HAD NO IDEA WAS GOING TO HAUNT ME MY ENTIRE LIFE UP UNTIL THE AGE OF 25. ME AND LECRAY WENT TO MEET UP WITH EVAN, EAZY, DEEDEE, AND LORD. WE ALL WERE LIKE A FAMILY SO I THOUGHT. UP UNTIL THIS NIGHT WE WERE ALL THICK AS THIEVES. WE ALL WERE IN LORD CAR SMOKING AND LECRAY SIAD THAT SHE WAS ABOUT TO GO BEFORE SHE GOT CAUGHT SNEAKING OUT. SHE ASKED ME DID I WANNA GO WITH HER AND I SAID NAW IM COOL IMA STAY A LIL LONGER THEY GONE DROP ME OFF AT THE CRIB IN A MINUTE. I DIDNT GO WITH HER AND SHE DIDNT THINK ANYTHING WOULD HAPPENED BUT IT DID. AFTER WE DRUNK A ENTIRE FIFTH OF HENNESSY WE

WENT TO THE LIQUOR STORE AGAIN ON DIXIE TO GET SOME MORE LIQUOR. EVAN AND LORD GOT OUT THE CAR TO GO IN THE STORE AND GET THE LIQUOR. ME EAZY AND DEEDEE SAT BACK IN THE CAR. EAZY WAS MY COUSIN LAURA BOYFRIEND AT THE TIME. DEEDEE I KNEW HIM THROUGH MY FIRST HIGH SCHOOL I WENT TO IN THE CITY. HE WAS IN THIS GANG WITH MY PLAY BROTHER SLEEPY CALLED THE DOME. WHEN THEY WENT INTO THE LIQUOR STORE I UESS DEEDEE THOUGHT IT WAS HIS CHANCE TO SHOOT HIS SHOT AT ME. HE SAID TO "SO YOU KNOW IM GETTING SOME OF YOU TONIGHT". I RESPONDED " PLEASE.. NEVER IN YOUR DREAMS SIR". AFTER I SAID THAT DEEDEE SAID "YEAH WE GONE SEE". LITTLE DID I KNOW I REALLY WAS ABOUT TO SEE. I ALSO WAS WONDERING WHY HE EVEN COMING AT ME IN THAT MANNER WHEN HE KNOW ME AND EVAN MESS WITH EACH OTHER. WE PARKED IN FRONT OF LORD HOUSE AND WAS LISTENING TO MUSIC AND SMOKING AND DRINKING. HE LIVED AROUND THE SORNER FROM MY MOM HOUSE SO I WASNT THAT FAR FROM HOME AND HE DATED MY FRIEND ON THE CHEERLEADING TEAM. SHANNON. WE THEN BEGAN TO START ON THE NEXT BOTTLE THIS TIME WE HAD A LEATER. AT THIS POINT I HAD TO MANY DRINKS AND WAS SIXTEEN DRINKING ALCOHOL UNDER AGE. MY PHONE WASNT RINGING KNOW ONE WAS LOOKING FOR ME SO I KEPT DRINKING. I THEN STARTED

TO BECOME DIZZY AND DIDNT REALIZE HOW MUCH ALCOHOL I HAD INTAKEN. I BLACKED OUT ALL I REMEBER IS WAKING UP TO THE SUN IN A ROOM THAT I HAD NO IDEA HOW I GOT IN. I WOKE UP TO A VERY HARSH BAD CRAMPING PAIN IN MY STOMACH. I ALSO WAS EXCESSIVELY BLEEDING FROM MY VAGINAL AREA AND STOOD UP AND SEEN THAT I HAD NO PANTS ON AND THE ROOM WAS GROCE. THERE WAS CONDOMS ALL OVER THE ROOM AND ALSO THERE WAS VOMIT ALL OVER THE FLOOR AND CUPS ANDEMPTY BOTTLES EVERYWHERE. I THEN RAN OUT THE ROOM SEEING EVANS PANTS PULLED DOWN AND HIM LAYING WRITE NEXT TO ME. ALSO DEEDEE WAS IN ANOTHER BED ACROSS FROM WERE ME AND EVAN WERE LAYING, HE WAS ASS NAKED. I HAD NO IDEA OR CLUE WHAT WAS GOING ON OR HOW I EVAN GOT TO A HOTEL. I THEN HAD A LIGHT POP IN MY HEAD AND I INSTANTLY WAS SCARED. THE SAME PERSON I HAD TOLD WASNT GETTING NONE OF ME ENDED UP GETTING SOME OF ME ANYWAY. I WAS TRYING TO UNDERSTAND WHY EVAN WOULD ALLOW SOMETHING LIKE THAT TO HAPPENED TO ME IF HE CARED ABOUT ME. HE REALLY DIDNT CARE IF HE WOULD HAVE SEX WITH ME AND LET HIS FRIEND AS WELL. NOW IM THINKING BUT WHAT IF I WAS SLEEP AND HE WAS AS WELL AND HE WAS TAKING ADVANTAGE OF ME. I ALSO THOUGHT THIS WAS MY PLAY BROTHERS FRIEND WHY WOULD HE TAKE

SOMETHING I MADE CLEAR I WASNT INTRESTED IN DOING. SO BECAUSE I WAS SO INTOXICATED AND WASNT GOING TO REMEBER I GUESS HE FIGURED THAT I WOULDNT SEE HIS ASS IN THE MORNING. WELL THEY DIDNT KNOW I WAS EVEN WOKE. DEEDEE SHOWED ME HE MENT WHAT HE SAID. I ASKED THE FRONT DESK CAN I USE THE PHONE TO CALL MY MOM SHE WAS YELLING AT ME AND WAS PIST OFF. SHE WOULDNT EVEN COME GET ME AFTER I TOLD HER I DIDNT KNOW WERE I WAS AND THAT I HAD BEEN RAPED AND WAS BLEEDING DOWN MY PANTS IN FRONT OF EVERYONE INTHE LOBBY. I STARTED WALKING UP THE ROAD TO THE POLICE STATION AND THIS LADY PULLED OVER BECAUSE SHE SEEN ME CRYING AND BLEEDING OUT OF MY PANTS REALLY BAD. SHE PULLED OVER AND ASKED ME WHAT MY MOM NUMBER WAS. SHE CALLED MY MOM TO STRESS THAT I WAS VERY MESSED UP AND BLEEDING BADLY AND SHE TOLD MY MOM TO MEET HER AT THE POLICE STATION. I WAS TERRIFIDE BUT AT THIS POINT IT DIDNT MATTER TO ME I WANTED TO GET AWAY FROM THAT SUPER 8 MOTEL BEFORE THEY WOKE UP AND DISCOVERED I WAS GONE. AFTER MY MOM SEEN THE BLOOD AND I TOLD HER WHAT HAPPENED SHE TOOK ME TO THE HOSPITAL TO GET A RAPE KIT PERFORMED ON ME. I HAD GOT ALCHOHOL POISINING SO I ENDED UP THROWING UP THE LINEN OF MY STOMACH I

THROUGH UP 7 BAGS OF STRAIGHT FLUID.. I CONSTANTLY WAS BLEEDING FROM MY VAGINAL AREA AND HAD NO CLUE WHY. THEY HAD DISCOVERED I WASNT ON MY PERIOD. AFTER RUNNING ALL THERE TEST THEY CAME BACK AND INFORMED ME THAT I HAD SCARRING AND SCRATCHES ON THE OUTSIDE OF MY VAGINAL AREA AND ON THE INSIDE OF MY VAGINAL ARE. I HAD BEEN TORN FROM THE INSIDE OF MY VAGINA AND THEY SAID THAT WHO EVER RAPED ME WAS VERY LARGE AND THATS WHY I HAVE SO MUCH SCARRING. WELL I THOUGHT TO MYSELF IT CANT BE EVAN BECAUSE I HAD ALREADY BEEN WITH HIM AND HIS PENNIS WAS SMALL AS EVER BAIRLY EVER STAYED IN THE HOT POCKET. SO IT COULD ONLY PERSON LEFT DEEDEE. I WENT TO SCHOOL WITH THESE GUYS AND WE LIVED IN THE SAME NEIGHBORHOOD WHY THEY DIDNT TAKE ME HOME AFTER THAT DAY I WILL NEVER KNOW. AT THIS POINT I DIDNT KNOW WHAT TO DO I WAS HURT AND EMBARESSED AND ASHAMED OF MYSELF ALL AT ONCE. I EVEN BLAMED MYSELF FOR WHY I GOT RAPED. IT WAS MY FAULT HONESTLY I FELT THE LORD PUNISHED ME THIS DAY FOR SNEAKING OUT WITHOUT TELLING MY MOM WERE I WAS GOING OR JUST BEING DISOBEDIANT ALL AROUND. I ALWAYS DID WHAT I WANTED NO MATTER WHAT ANOTHER PERSON TOLD ME NOT TO DO. I STAYED HOME FOR THREE MONTHS AND DIDNT COME OUT MY ROOM

FOR DAYS. I SLEPT ALL DAY AND I WAS SO TORN I WAS BLEEDING FOR A MONTH STRAIGHT. I WOULD STARE AT THE WALLA ND NOT DO ANYTHING AND KEEP MY BLINDS CLOTHES. MY MOM WOULD HERE ME CRY FOR WEEKS AND WHEEP FOR WEEKS. I DIDNT GO BACK TO SCHOOL UNTIL IT WAS TIME TO TAKE S.A.T'Z. I WASNT READY FOR THIS. THE POLICE HAD FOLLOWED BACK UP WITH ME AND INSTRUCTED ME TO NOT PRESS CHARGES ON THEM BECAUSE OF HOW MANY OF THEM IT WAS AND THEY ALL WILL RIP ME TO PIECES ON A STAND AND MAKE ME LOOK LIKE A SLUT BECAUSE ITS MY WORD AGAINST THERES. HE SAID I DIDNT EVEN HAVE A CASE. I REGRET NOT PRESSING CHARES BECAUSE AFTER ME I FOUND OUT DEEDEE HAD DONE THAT TO SEVERAL OTHER FEMALES BEFORE ME. THE OLDER I GOT I HAD HURD FROM A SOURCE IN DEEDEE CIRCLE HE DID IT TO ANOTHER WOMAN AFTER ME. WHAT DO U DO WHEN YOU FEAR WHAT WILL HAPPEN TO YOU AND YOUR GOOD REP. I WAS WORRIED ABOUT BEING JUDGED FOR THE FIRST TIME IN MY LIFE. I LEARNED A LESSON OF LOVE,LOYALTY, RESPECT, AND TRUST FOR MYSELF. I ALSO LEARNED YOU CAN CALL SOMEONE YOUR FRIEND AND THEY STILL ARENT YOUR FRIEND UNTIL THEY PROVE IT TO YOU. I ALSO LEARNED THAT JUST BECAUSE YOU THINK A GUY WONT TAKE IT NEVER PUT IT PASSED THEM. I HAD BEEN DEGRADED IN THE WORSE

WAY BY PEOPLE I TOUGHT WERE MY FRIEND. THE POLICE OFFICER MAD ME FEEL LIKE MY VOICE DIDNT MATTER., NO ONE WILL EVER HERE ME, NO ONE WILL EVER LISTEN TO ME, NO ONE WILL EVER SEE ME,NO ONE WILL EVER BELIEVE ME. MY TRUTH IS MINE THOUGH AND I FORGIVE THE PEOPLE IN THE SITUATION THAT WAS INVOLVED WITH ONE PERSON OUT OF THE BUNCH PROBLEM THEY CREATED FOR THEMSELVES. THERE RAPEST AMONG YOUR CHILDREN EVEN IN HIGH SCHOOL IS ANOTHER LESSON I LEARNED.

ANXIETY AFTER RAPE

NOW I HAVE TO DEAL WITH PEOPLE LOOKING AT ME ODD AND HAVING THERE OWN PERSONAL OPINION OF WHAT HAPPEN TO ME. I ASKED JOANN IF WE COULD MOVE AWAY AND SHE SAID YES. I ALSO ASKED CAN I TRANSFER TO ANOTHER SCHOOL. I DIDNT CARE ABOUT THE FRIENDSHIPS I HAD MADE WITH PEOPLE OR ANY TYPE OF BONDS I HAD CREATED WITH PEOPLE. I ALSO WS A MEMBER OF THE BLOODS AT THIS TIME I DIDNT CARE ABOUT ANY OF THAT AND I JUST WANTED TO LEAVE THE ENTIRE ENVIORNMENT. JOANN SEEN HOW HURT AND EMOTINALLY DRAINED I WAS AND I HONESTLY THINK SHE FELT PITTY AND SORRY FOR ME ANYWAY. I ALSO WAS VERY SUICIDEL AND I HAD STARTED BLAMING MYSELF AGAIN FOR OTHER PEOPLES ACTIONS. I FELT IT WAS MY FAULT WHAT HAD HAPPENED TO ME, I REALIZED I HAD NEEDED MORE PYSCHOLOGICAL HELP THEN I THOUGHT I DID. ALL SUMMER I DIDNT DO ANYTHING BUT PREPARE MYSELF FOR A NEW START. MY MOTHER WHEN WE MOVED FELT SHE WAS PROTECTING ME. SHE TAUGHT ME TO RUN AWAY FROM MY PROBLEMS AND FROM

CONFLICT BY AGREEING TO MOVE. SHE JUST WAS TRYNA MAKE HER DAUGHTER HAPPY AGAIN SO I COULDNT BLAME HER. WE MOVE TO THE OTHERSIDE OF HAZEL CREST WITH THE BIGGER HOUSES AND NICER NEIGHBORHOOD. I THEN STARTED TO GO TO HILLCREST HIGH SCHOOL. I STARTED SNEAKING BACK IN THE CITY ON MY OWN WITH MY REBELIOUS SELF. I DIDNT WANNA MAKE FRIENDS I JUST MISSED THE FRIENDS I HAD SINCE I WAS A KID. I WOULD GO KICK IT OVER EAST IN THE HUNNIDS AND MOE TOWN. I THEN MET THIS GUY NAME ALLEN WHEN I WAS GOING INTO THE CITY ONE DAY. I WAS GETTING OFF THE BUS AND HE PULLED UP IN A MERCEDES BEINS AND ASKED ME TO GET IN. AFTER WHAT JUST HAPPENED TO ME U WOULD THINK I WOULDNT BUT I DID. I DID GET IN THE CAR WITH HIM BECAUSE I TOLD MYSELF IF ANYONE EVER TRIED TO TAKE SOMETHING FROM ME I WOULD COMPLY WITH THEM AND MURDER THEM IN THE PROCESS. MY MIND WAS GROWING DARKER AND DARKER. THE WILLINGNESS TO HURT SOMEONE EVERYDAY GREW IN MY SPIRIT. THIS GUY TREATED ME WITH SO MUCH LOVE THAT I HAD NEVER FELT BEFORE. LITTLE DID I KNOW EVERYTHING THAT GLITTERS ISNT GOLD. MY MOM STOPPED CARRING SO MUCH ABOUT ME GOING OUTSIDE A LITTLE BIT AFTER ALL I WAS 18 AT THIS POINT. ON AUGUST 23RD HE TOOK ME UP TO THIS APARTMENT . IT SMELLED LIKE DEATH. I

THEN TURNED MY HEAD AND NEXT THING YOU KNOW HE WAS BULTING THE DOOR DOWN. I THOUGHT THE HORROR ENDED WHEN I MOVED BUT IT DIDNT. HE THEN SAID TO ME YOU STUCK HERE FOREVER. YOU NOT GOING BACK HOME TO YOUR MOM AND YOUR MINE FOREVER. CHILLS RAN THROUGH MY BODY. I DIDNT PANIC I JUST WAS THINKING THAT I WAS IN HELL ON EARTH. NEVER KNEW SOMEONE WHO SHOWED ME SO MUCH LOVE AND CARE WOULD TRY AND HOLD ME HOSTAGE. HE THEN ASKED ME TO TAKE ALL MY CLOTHES OFF. I DID AS I WAS TOLD. HE THEN PENATRATED ME AND I DIDINT WANT IT. I LAYED THERE CRYING AND SHIVERING NOT KNOWING IF I WAS GOING TO LIVE OR DIE AFTER HE WAS FINISHED DOING HIS BUSINESS. DAY 2 HE FED ME AND I DIDNT EAT ALL DAY WHEN HE WOULD LOCK ME IN. THE FOOD HE GAVE ME WAS BROCCOLI CARROTS AND LETTUCE NO DRESSING. THAT SHIT WAS GROCE. HE TOLD ME IF HE EVER CAUGHT ME EATING MEET HE WOULD KILL ME. DAY THREE HE CAME BACK THE NEXT DAY AND MADE ME SCRUB THE FLOORS. HE SAT IN THE CHAIR WITH A SINISTER LOOK ON HIS FACE EATING A APPLE. I DID WHATEVER HE ASKED ALL BECAUSE I KNEW IF I DIDNT ADAPT TO THE ENVIRONMENT THAT I AM IN THAT I WOULD BE KILLED FOR BEING BEAUTIFUL. I SEEN HE JUST WANTED TO CONTROL SOMEONE SO I GAVE HIM THE CONTROL. HE WOULD LET ME

TALK TO MY FRIENDS AND FAMILY AND HE ONLY GAVE ME FIVE MINUTES A PEACE WITH THEM. HE TOOK ME TO SCHOOL AND PICKED ME UP AND IF I WASNT ON TIME HE WOULD COME LOOKING FOR ME AND HE WOULD FIND ME. SO EAR OF HIM FINDING ME AND MY FAMILY WAS WHAT KEPT ME QUIET FROM TELLING ANYONE WHAT WAS GOING ON WITH ME. HE CHOSE ME FOR A REASON. THE ONLY REASON WAS THAT HE SEEN I FEARED HIM. HE WAS 29 I WAS 18. DAY FOUR I DIDNT GET TO GO TO SCHOOL HE WOKE ME UP DID HIS BUSINESS ON ME AND THEN TOOK ME TO THE BATH TUB TO WASH ME UP. HE SAID I WAS HIS FAVORITE ONE AS HE BAITHED ME AND HE SAID THAT NO ONE WOULD EVER TAKE MY PLACE. I STARTED TO LOOK AROUND FOR SOMETHING TO HIT HIM WITH AND KNOCK HIM OUT FOR GOOD. I COULDNT FIND ANYTHING HE DIDNT LEAVE ANYTHING I COULD TURN INTO A WEAPON. I VALUED BEING HOME MORE AFTER BEING SOME WHERE I DIDNT WANNA BE. DAY FIVE CAME AND HE GOT TO COMFOTORABLE AND TRUSTING TOWARD ME. I HAD BEAT HIM AT HIS OWN GAME. I HAD MADE HIM TRUST ME TO THE POINT WERE HE WOULD MAKE A SIMPLE MISTAKE LIKE LIVING A WINDOW OPEN IN THE BATHROOM AFTER HE GOT OUT THE SHOWER. HE RAN OUT THE HOUSE IN A RUSH BECAUSE SOMEONE HAD GOT IN HIS STASH HE HAD TO GO CHECK AND MAKE SURE EVERYTHING WAS O.K AT HIS OTHER

PROPERTY. I THEN BROKE THE HANDLE YOU USE TO OPEN THE STOVE OFF THE STOVE. I PRIDE OPEN THE BACKROOM DOOR THINKING IT WAS A BACK DOOR TRYING TO FINALLY GET AWAY.HE HAD FOUR BODIES IN A ROOM ONCE I GOT IN THROUGH THE DOOR. THEY WERE ALL BLOODIE AND DECOMPOSING. ONE WAS A FRESH BODY. I STOOD IN SHOCK AT WHAT I HAD SEEN I DIDNT VOMIT OR CRY AT THE SICKESS SHIT I HAD EVER SEEN IN MY LIFE. TWO OF THERE HEADS HAD BIG HOLES IN THEM. I RN INTO THE BATHROOM SCREAMING I DROPPED TWO PILLOWS OUT THE WINDOW. I KNEW I WAS HIGH UP I DIDNT GIVE A SHIT. HE WASNT GOING TO DO TO ME WHAT I SEEN HIM DO TO THOSE FOUR YOUNG GIRLS. GOD WAS WITH ME WHEN I JUMPED I DIDNT BREAK NOT ONE LIMB. I HAD JUMPED ALMOST 15 FEET OUT OF THE AIR. I RAN TO THE NEAREST BUS AND GOT OFF ON 147TH STREET AND MY MALE FRIEND TEACE HAD CAME TO PICK ME UP. I USE TO RUN WITH TEACE HE TAUGHT ME HOW TO SELL DOPE , MAKE IT AND MORE,AND ANYTIME I GOT IN TROUBLE HE WOULD BOND ME OUT OF JAIL AND HAD MONEY TO EXPUNDGE MY RECORD IF NEED BE. WHY HE ALWAYS HELPED ME I DONT KNOW I THINK HE HAD A LOVE FOR ME I DIDNT KNOW. I WAS SUPPOSED TO BE AT MY FRIENDS HOUSE SO MY MOM DIDNT KNOW ANYTHING THAT HAD JUST WENT ON. I WAS GOING TO MAKE IT MY BUSINESS THAT SHE NEVER FOUND OUT. TEICE

CALLED THE POLICE TO WEAR I WAS BEING HELD AND JUST THERE LUCK HE WAS PULLING UP. THE TOOK THE BODIES OUT AND ARRESTED HIM FOR ONLY THE GIRLS WHO WERE IN THE HOUSE. I TOLD TEICE TO TAKE THE FALL I DIDNT WANT THEM TO KNOW THAT I WAS IN THAT HOUSE AS WELL WITH THOSE BODIES. MY BIRTHDAY CAME UP AND I COULDNT BE MORE GRATEFUL. I WENT TO DERRICK HOUSE THE NEXT DAY WE HAD JUST GOT BACK ON TALKING TERMS AND HE HAD BOUGHT ME MY FIRST CAR. I DIDNT SAY ANYTHING TO MY DAD OUT OF FEAR OF DISAPPOINTING MY DAD. HE NEVER WAS HAPPY WITH ME AND SEEING HIM HAPPY IN THAT MOMENT I DIDNT WANT TO TAKE THAT AWAY FROM HIM. BY THEN I HAD LEARNED HOW TO CONTROL NOT SHOWING WHAT I WAS FEELING. I ALSO STOPPED CARING WHAT PEOPLE THOUGHT OF ME AS WELL. I HAD OVERSHADOWED THE DARKNESS WITH THE BRIGHT LIGHT HAD GIVEN ME IN MY SOUL. I WAS SUPPOSED TO LIVE AND BE HERE. AFTER THAT REALIZATION I WASNT INTRESTED IN THE REBEL LIFESTYLE ANYMORE. I WAS READY TO STEP INTO THE WORLD WITH ALL THE BAGGAGE AND PASS MISTAKES. A ENERGY CAME OVER MY BODY. I HAD THEN GRADUATED AND STARTED A NEW LIFE WITH MY HIGH SCHOOL SWEETHEART THAT I HAD MET WHILE ATTENDING SCHOOL AT HILL CREST HIGH SCHOOL.

NEW WORLD

I HAD FOUND MY WAY BACK TO MYSELF. MY BOYFRIEND WHO WAS A BIG TIME CARD CRACKER IN COUNTRY CLUB HILLS AREA AT THE TIME WAS MY BESTFRIEND. WE DID EVERYTHING TOGETHER. I ALSO HAD MET MY FEMALE BESTFRIEND OF A LIFETIME MY LAST YEAR OF HIGH SCHOOL AS WELL. DEASHAUN WAS MY BOYFRIEND AND CRAY WAS MY BESTFRIEND I FELT AS IF THEY WERE ALL I NEEDED IN MY LIFE. I THEN WAS TRYING TO GET INTO COLLEGE. I WANTED TO GO TO THE ART INSTITUTE FOR PHOTOGRAPHY. MY DAD DIDNT FOLLOW THROUGH WHEN IT CAME TIME TO PAY SO HE HELPED CRUSH MY DREAM BEFORE I COULD EVEN BE A NUMBER ONE PHOTOGRAPHER IN CHICAGO IL. THAT WAS WHAT I ASPIRED TO BE AND HE WANTED ME TO WORK IN THE MEDICAL FIELD, SO DID MY MOM. ME AND JOANN ENDED UP GOING TO DEVRY UNIVERSITY IN MARRIONETTE PARK ILLINOIS. I SEEN PHARMACY TECHNICIAN AND I HAD ALWAYS WANTED TO BE ONE. I THOUGHT THAT PILLS AND BLOOD WERE ALWAYS FASINATING TO ME. I KNOW IT SOUNDS A LITTLE COOKY BUT ITS MY TRUTH.

WE GOT ALL THE WAY THROUGH THE PROCESS AND I WAS EXCITED THEN WE GET TO THE PAY PART AGAIN. SHE DIDNT WANT TO PAY JUST LIKE MY DAD DIDNT. MY PARENTS BOTH WERE SUCCESSFUL AND ALWAY BRAGGED ABOUT THEM WANTING ME AND MY BROTHERS TO BE GREAT. THEY WERE LAZY ABOUT HELPING ME BECOME WHO THEY WANTED ME TO BE BASED OFF THE WAY THEY CAME UP IN LIFE. MY EDUCATION WASNT EVEN AS IMPORTANT TO THEM AS THEY HAD STRESSED IT TO BE.HONESTLY I FELT THEY WANTED TO HELP ME FAIL IN LIFE. I THEN GOT A JOB WORKING AT NORTHWESTERN HOSPITAL ON THE SECOND FLOOR IN AU BON PAIN CAFE AND BAKERY. I HAD NEVER IN LIFE THOUGHT I WOULD BE WORKING IN THE SAME PLACE MY MOM HAD WORKED ALL MY LIFE GROWING UP. I LOVED MY JOB BUT ME AND MY MOM RELATIONSHIP WAS ON A DOWN SPIRAL. IM NOW 19 AND ME AND DEASHAUN ARE STILL TOGETHER. I DIDNT HAVE MUCH TIME TO GO ON RUNS WITH HIM ANYMORE SO ME AND HIM GREW A LITTLE DISTANT BECAUSE OF ME WORKING. I DIDNT HAVE AS MUCH TIME FOR MY BABY NO MORE. LATER DOWN THE LINE ME AND HIS SONS MOM CAUGHT HIM UP TOGETHER AFTER SHE HAD SHOWED ME A VIDEO OF HIM HAVING SEX WITH HER. I DUMPED HIM AND WE PARTED WAYS. MY MOM KICKED ME OUT BECAUSE AFTER GRADUATION I BAIRLEY WOULD EVEN COME

IN THE HOUSE. SHE ALSO KEPT A CURFUEW OF 1 OCLOCK ON ME. I WASNT HAVEN THAT BULLSHIT. I WAS TO BUSY KICKING IT WITH ALL THE BALLERS THROUGH CHICAGO AND DAMN NEAR ALL THE GANG MEMBERS THAT I CONSIDERED FAMILY. I THEN STARTED TO DEVELOP AND NAME AND A FACE FOR MYSELF IN THESE STREETS. IT WAS ALWAYS POSITIVE BUT I WOULD DO THINGS FOR GANGS SO THAT I COULD HAVE PROTECTION AND SO THAT I COULD HAVE RESPECT. BEING LOVED BY MEMBERS WAS A DIFFERENT TYPE OF LOVE. WE ALL WERE HURT PEOPLE IN SOME WAY SO WE SHARED THAT FEELING OF EMPTYNESS. I TOLD MY SELF IM ABOUT TO MAKE MYSELF A CHI-TOWN QUEEN.

20 IN THE STREETS

NOW IM THE BIG TWO ZERO, ME AND DEASHAUN HAD GOT BACK TOGETHER. I COULDNT TAKE THE HARSH STREET SHIT LIVING HOUSE TO HOUSE IT WAS IRRITATING A LIL BIT. WE BOTH WERE AT THE SAME GAS STATION ONE DAY AND THAT HOW WE GOT BACK INTUNE WITH EACH OTHER. I SEEN HIM THAT DAY AND STARTED TO REMANINCE ABOUT THE GOOD TIMES WE HAD AND THE WONDERFUL SEX WE HAD. THE NEXT DAY I WENT TO SEE HIM AND FROM THAT NEXT DAY IT WAS UP FROM THERE. NEITHER ONE OF US CARED IF EITHER OF US WERE DEALING WITH ANYONE ALL WE HAD NEW IS WE MISSED THAT LOVE WE USE TO GIVE EACH OTHER ALL THE TIME. NO FIGHTS NO HURT FEELINGS JUST STRAIGHT LAUGHTER. HE THEN WENT TO JAIL AND MY LIFE TURNED UPSIDE DOWN. I WAS LIVING WITH HIM AT THE TIME WHEN HE WENT TO JAIL. HIS MOTHER WAS PHONY SO WHEN HE GOT LOCKED UP I HAD TO GO AS WELL. I THEN WENT TO STAY WITH MY SISTERS FROM OVER EAST IN NOB HILL A NEIGHBORHOOD IN COUNTRY CLUB HILL ILLINOIS. ONE NAME WAS STARBURST AND THE

OTHER HER NAME WAS MOON. THEY LET ME STAY AS LONG AS I NEEDED TO. I THEN DISCOVERED HE WAS CHEATING ON ME AGAIN. WHEN HE WENT TO JAIL I WENT TO THE MARKHAM COURTHOUSE AND HE GAVE ME HIS PHONE. HE SAID WHATEVER YOU SEE IN THIS PHONE DONT PAY ATTENTION TO IT I WILL BE GOING TO JAIL IMA CALL MY PHONE ANSWER AND HE GAVE ME THE PASSWORD TO THE PHONE. THE THINGS I SEEN AFTER I LOOKED ANYWAY WERE UNBAIRABLE. THE VIDEOS, THE PICTURES OF MULTIPLE DIFFERENT WOMEN BODY PARTS, THE MESSAGES I WAS SEEING THAT WERE DEEP WITH CERTAIN FEMALES. WAS SICKENING TO ME. HOW COULD U BE SO DISHONEST AND CLAIM YOU LOVE ALL OVER 20 OF THESE FEMALES U CLAIM TO LOVE IN YOUR PHONE. I WAS PISSED MY DUMB ASS HAD JUST TATTED HIS NAME ON ME SOON AS HE WENT TO JAIL. I WAS HOMELESS AND I WAS STILL CRACKING WHATEVER MOVES HE HAD LEFT IN HIS PHONE FOR HIM. IM HOMELESS SUPPORTING A MAN INCARSERATED BECAUSE OF DECISIONS HE MADE AND HE NOT EVEN IN LOVE WITH ME. I ACTED AS IF I DIDNT SEE ANY OF THE STUFF AND I WENT FOR MY REVENGE. I LIVED BY YOU DO WRONG TO ME I DO WRONG TO YOU NO MATTER WHAT THE CIRCUMSTANCES ARE. I WAS SO HURT AND TORN SO I MOVED AWAY TO INDIANAPPOLIS INDIANA. I TOLD MY MOM WHAT HAD HAPPENED AND I TOLD HER I

FELT LIKE KILLING SOMEONE AND SHE CAME AND GOT ME. THAT DAY SHE SAVED ME BECAUSE IF I WOULD HAVE STAYED IN ILLINOIS AFTER ALL THE TRAUMA I HAD BEEN THROUGH OR IF I HAD STAYED KNOWING THE THINGS I KNOW AND HAVING THESE HOES ADDRESSES THEN I WOULD HAVE HAD THEM KILLED. JUST WHEN I THOUGHT THE PAIN WAS OVER I WENT TO THE DOCTOR DOWN THERE JUST TO GET HURT SOME MORE. AL THE CHEATING HE HAD GOING ON HAD A LITTLE RAPED PACKAGE WITH THE CHEATING AS WELL.HE HAD GAVE ME CHLAMIDIA AND TRICAMONIST AND GOHNARIA ALL AT ONCE. I WANTED TO KILL HIM AND EVER SINGLE WOMEN HE HAD SLEPT WITH ON ME. I THEN STOPPED DATING AND GOT A JOB AND A CAR AND MY FIRST OWN APARTMENT. THINGS WERE ON THE UP AND OUT. I THEN STARTED TO GET A BIGGER BAG THEN EVER BEFORE. I ALSO HAD LEARNED MY WAY AROUND THE NAP PRETTY GOOD. I THEN STARTED WORKING IN THE MALL AS A JANITOR. I ONE DAY WAS IN THE MALL AND I WAS CLEANING OFF THE TABELS IN THE FOOD COURT WITH MY COWORKER DANA.AND THESE TWO SUPER TALL GUYS WALKED UP TO ME AND MY FRIEND. I WASNT INTRESTED IN NO GUY AT ALL I JUST WANTED TO MIND MY BUSINESS. DANA ASKED THEM WHAT YALL WANT ARE NUMBER OR SOMETHIN? SHE ASKED THAT BECAUSE THEY WERE GLOATING OVER US. I

HAD NEVER SEEN ANYONE TAKE INTREST IN A JANITOR IN THE MALL BUT WE BOTH WERE FINE ADN THICK AS FUCK. NEXT THING I KNOW HIS FRIEND WALKS UP AND SAYS YOUR THE ONE I WANT. HE SMILED AT MEAND I CRACKED UP LAUGHHING. HE SAID "YEAH YOU GIRL, I WANT YO". I WAS SHOCKED, THEY WERE BOTH FINE AS HELL AND LOOKED LIKE NBA BASKETBALL PLAYERS. HE THEN REPONDED WHATS YOUR NAME? WHO AM I LOOKING AT? I THEN RESPONDED BOY PLEASE I DONT WANT NO SMOKE WITH YOU SIR. HE PROCEEDED TO ASK ME "WERE YOU FROM?, I HERE A ACCENT. YOU MUST NOT BE FROM HERE"? I SAID I FROM CHICAGO AND WE DONT CARRY A ACCENT SORRY YOU CANT HEAR THAT PART THROUGH YOUR BIG ASS EARS. AS YOU CAN SEE I HAD NO FILTER ON MY TOUNG. HE SAID HOW ABOUT I MAKE A DEAL WITH YOU? I RESPONDED "LIKE WHAT"? HE ASKED" LET ME BUY YOU LUNCH FOR THIRTY DAYS AND IF U LIKE ME AFTER THE THIRTY DAYS THEN I ET TO TAKE YOU ON A DATE". I THOUGHT ABOUT IT AND OF COURSE I LOVE FOOD SO I SAID YES. I THOUGHT HE WAS BULLSHITTING BUT HE WASNT HE QUICKLEY SHOWED ME. THIS MAN REALLY BOUGHT ME FOOD EVERYDAY FOR LUNCH. I HAD NEVER SEEN A MAN BE SO CONSISTANT. THIS WAS DIFFERENT FROM WHAT I WAS USE TO. HIS NAME WAS CAIN AND HE CAME FROM A VERY HIGH PROFILE GANG FAMILY IN ATLANTA. HE ALSO WAS A MUSIC

PRODUCER AND BIG TIME DRUG KINGPIN WHEN I MET HIM. HE WAS 6 FOOT 6 AND HE LOOKED ALMOST IDENTICAL TO WILL SMITH WITH THE EARS AND EVERYTHING ELSE THAT WERE HIS FEATURES. DAY 30 CAME AND HE ASKED ME CAN HE HAVE HIS DATE NOW. HE KEPT COUNT I WAS IMPRESSED. WE THEN WENT TO THE DRIVE IN MOVIES OUT TO EAT AND THEN HE TOOK ME BACK HOME.AS MORE AND MORE TIME PASSED WE BECAME A ITEM AND HE HAD MY HEART. HE WOULD COME OVER ALL THE TIME UNTIL I STARTED TO NOTICE HE WOULDNT ANSWER CERTAIN CALLS AND HE WOULD IGNORE CERTAIN FEMALES WHO WERE CALLING HIM. I ASKED BECAUSE THIS ONE NUMBER JUST KEPT CALLING. HIS RESPONSE TO ME ABOUT WHO IT WAS IS THAT IT WAS A FEMALE HE WAS DEALING WITH BEFORE ME TRYING TO CLAIM THAT SHE HAD A BABY ON THE WAY WITH HIM. WE THEN STARTED TO HAVE SEX TWO DAYS AFTER HIM TELLING ME THIS. HE SAID HE WANTED A BABY BY ME AND I SAID THATS FINE AS LONG AS YOUR GOING TO TAKE CARE OF IT. I ALSO HAD TOLD HIM I COULDNT GET PREGNANT FROM WHAT HAD HAPPENED TO ME IN HIGH SCHOOL WICH WAS A FACT THAT I HAD FOUND OUT LATER ON THROUGH MY DOCTOR.HE THEN INSERTED HIMSELF INSIDE ME AND I HAD NEVER FELT A DICK THAT BIG IN MY LIFE. I ALSO HAD NEVER HAD ANYONE MAKE ME CRY WHILE HAVING SEX OUT OF

LOVE. I FELT HIS SEEMEN SHOOT IN MY STOMACH AND A TEAR FELL FROM MY EYE. HE LOOKED ME IN MY EYES WHEN HE NUTTED IN ME. I WAS DEEPER IN LOVE BECAUSE HE HAD MADE ME FEEL A CERTAIN WAY SEXUALLY I HAD NEVER FELT BEFORE. ONLY THING I HATED WAS HIS DICK WAS EXTREMELY LARGE I WASNT TRYNA MAKE IT A HABBIT SITTING ON THAT DINASOUR OF HIS IS WHAT I CALLED IT. AFTER HE NUTTED IN ME HE GOT COMFOTRABLE. STARTED LEAVING THINGS OVER MY HOUSE ON PURPOSE WASNT BUYING NICE THINGS ANYMORE OR TAKING ME ON NICE DATES. HE ALSO STOPPED COMING OVER ALL THE TIME. HE ALSO TURNED INTO A DIFFERENT MAN I HAD NEVER MET BEFORE. I THEN STOPPED LIKING HIM AND DUMPED HIS ASS. I CAUGHT HIM CHEATING IN THE APPLEBEES LITERALLY RIGHT AROUND THE CORNER FROM MY HOUSE WICH WAS IN TURTLE CREEK APARTMENTS.I THEN TOLD HIM I JUST WANTED TO REMAIN FRIENDS AND DIDNT WANNA HAVE SEX OR BE WITH HIM ANYMORE. HE HAD ALREADY HAD ANOTHER CHILD IN ATLANTA THAT WAS 6 AT THE TIME. HE HAD TO MUCH GOING ON AND WAS STARTING TO LOOK LIKE A ISTAKE. HE WOULD CONTINUE TO COME OVER AFTER THAT BUT WE WOULD JUST WATCH MOVIES AND SMOKE. WE ONLY HAD SEX TWO TIMES EVER IN LIFE AND NEVER DID IT AGAIN. HIS BIRTHDAY WAS COMING UP AND CAIN WAS TURNING 27. HIS

BIRTHDAY WAS NOVEMBER 7TH AND MY BIRTHDAY WAS NOVEMEBER 23RD. I REALIZED THAT A SCORPIO AND SAGGITARRIOUS DONT MIX ANYWAY. I TOLD HIM HAPPY BIRTHDAY AND HAD GOT HIM A BOTTLE AND COOKED FOR HIM AND GAVE HIM A 3.5 FOR HIS BIRTHDAY. I MADE SURE I MADE IT MY BUSINESS TO FIND OUT WHY I HAVENT CAME ON MY PERIOD. I WAS 5 DAYS LATE AFTER ALL. I URINATED ON A AT HOME TEST TWO DAY BEFORE MY BIRTHDAY IT SAID I WAS PREGNAT. I THOUGHT TO MYSELF I CANT BE. I TOOK ANOTHER ONE BOTH SAID I WAS PREGNANT. I SENT THE TEST TO CAIN AND I DIDNT EXPECT TO GET THE REACTION I DID. HE SAID WHAT THATS SUPPOSED TO MEAN. HE THOUGHT THE TEST WASNT REAL HE TOLD ME GO GET A ULTRASOUND. I WENT AND DID JUST THAT AND I GOT TO SEE THE FIRST LOVE OF MY LIFE EVER.IT WAS A LITTLE WORM LOOKING THING SWIMMING AROUND IN THIS LITTLE CIRCLE. THE DOCTOR SAID I WAS 6 WEEKS PREGNAT. I TOLD CAIN AND HE SAID I NEEDED TO GET A ABORTION. I SAID IF THAT WHAT HE WANTS THAT FINE I WILL BOOK THE APPOINTMENT AND YOUR GOING TO PAY FOR IT. HE SAID HE WASNT AND I RESPONDED WELL IM KEEPING IT THEN BECAUSE IM NOT PAYING FOR A SIN I DONT WANT TO COMMIT IN THE FIRST PLACE. HE SCREAMED AT ME IN THE PHONE AND INSINUATED THAT I TRIED TO RUIN HIS LIFE. HE THEN STARTED TO OPEN PANDORAS BOX

AND TELL THE TRUTH. AFTER ALL HIS LYING HE WAS DOING HE HAD GIVEN UP ON DIGGING A BIGGER WHOLE FOR HIS SELF. HE SAID THAT THE GIRL REALLY WAS PREGNANT AND THE FEMALE IN ATLANTA HE HAD THE 6 YEAR OLD BY SHE AND HIM WERE GETTING BACK TOGETHER AND HE WAS MOVING BACK TO ATLANTA. I SAID THATS FINE I JUST WANT U TO RAISE YOUR KID I HAVE NOTHING TO DO WITH YOUR RELATIONSHIP LETS JUST CO PARENT AND BE GOOD FRIENDS. HE BECAME IN RADGE AND SAID YOUR GOING TO RAISE THAT BABY ALONE. HE SAID HE WAS CHANGING HIS PHONE NUMBERS AND HIS LOCATION OF WERE HE LIVED. I THEN SEEN HIM WHILE I WAS SEVEN MONTHS PREGNANT AFTER HE HAD CHANGED HIS NUMBER AND CLAIMED TO MOVE BACK TO THE A.I YELLED HIS NAME OUT IN THE STORE AND HE WAS BUYING NEWBORN PAMPERS FOR THE BABY THATS TWO OR THREE MONTHS OLDER THEN THE ONE HE WAS GOING TO HAVE WIT ME. AFTER I CALLED HIS REAL NAME ERIC, HIS HEAD TURNED AND LOOKED AT ME AND MY BELLY AND HE DROPPED THE PAMPERS AND RAN OUT THE STORE. I WANTED TO KNOW WHY HE RAN AND I SEEN WHY HE HAD THE BABY AND THE GIRL IN THE CAR WITH HIM. I WASNT HURT ABOUT THE OTHER KID I WAS HURT THAT HE CHOSE TO SAY FUCK THE KID HE CREATED INSIDE OF ME. I EVENTUALLY LEARNED IT WAS WORTH IT. ON JULY 19TH,2015

MY LIFE CHANGED FOREVER. AFTER 48 HOURS OF HARD LABOR MY BEAUTIFUL SON TRISTAN D.ARMSTRONG WAS BOR 7 POUNDS AND 6 OUNCES AND 20 INCHES LONG. I LOOKED INTO HIS GREY EYES AND I KNEW I WOULD NEVER CARE ABOUT ANOTHER MAN AGAIN. I CARED ABOUT HIM BEING LOVE PROPERLY. NOW I HAD SOMEONE WHO LOVE WILL NEVER LEAVE ME AND I HAD SOMEONE WHO WILL FOREVER EXCEPT ALL THE LOVE I GIVE HIM.

A STAR IS BORN

TO BE CONTINUED

www.ingramcontent.com/pod-product-compliance
Lightning Source LLC
LaVergne TN
LVHW091209180726
843490LV00007B/2672